*I*mpossible is an *I*llusion

By Paul Semendinger, Ed.D.

RESOURCE *Publications* • Eugene, Oregon

Resource Publications
A division of Wipf and Stock Publishers
199 W 8th Ave, Suite 3
Eugene, OR 97401

Impossible is an Illusion
By Semendinger, Paul
Copyright©2017 by Semendinger, Paul
ISBN 13: 978-1-5326-7218-7
Publication date 10/6/2018
Previously published by Ravenswood Publishing, 2017

With Thanks and Appreciation…

How does a person find the words to thank the many special people who have been so instrumental in his life?

To Laurie, you are the love of my life. You always knew I'd be a writer. I cannot thank you enough for always being by my side, always listening to my stories, and being the rock that I rely on. Thanks for being a contributor, and editor, and critic. You are my best friend. The first best day in my life was meeting you, each day after has been an even better day. You are my wife, my best friend, and, most importantly, the best mom to our wonderful three boys. I love you!

To Ryan, Alex, and Ethan, I am, as Lou Gehrig once said, *"The Luckiest Man on the face of the Earth."* That is because I am the father of the three most wonderful sons in the whole world. I have written hundreds of thousands of words in my life and yet none can ever fully explain the deep love, affection, and respect I have for each of you. You make me proud each and every day. You are each, quite simply, the best.

I am very fortunate to have the greatest parents in the world. Mom and Dad, I love you. Thanks for always believing in me and teaching me that I really can do anything. I wouldn't be who I am today without you.

To my mother-in-law and father-in-law, thank you for always pushing me to be the very best. Your support always makes a positive difference in all our lives. We have enjoyed so many great memories together. I love you.

We are, in a way, the sum total of all those who have impacted on our lives. Thank you to my sister Laura, my grandparents, my uncles, aunts, cousins, nieces, and nephews who share their happiness, joy, and love with me. I have always looked up to my cousin David

Semendinger. Virginia is just too far away, and time too fleeting... I am a very fortunate person indeed to have such a family.

In my career, I have worked with so many outstanding teachers that it would be impossible to list them all – the people, who from the very start, encouraged and championed me and helped make me an educator. Mrs. Pinkos and Mrs. Williams will always hold special places in my heart. Margy, Bill, Dave, Charlie, and Norman were there with me at the start. Boy did we have a lot of laughs and good times together. We were also the greatest teaching team in the history of... forever. I still miss those wonderful days together in Fair Lawn. Go Olympians!

I had the great fortune of working for three of the greatest principals of all time: Mr. Miller, Mr. Kane, and Mr. Fisher. Each was always there for me. They helped me believe that someday I might be able to do the same job that they did. I have attained the same position, but I am not, and never will be, the leaders they were.

At Hawes Elementary School, I work with the most amazing staff ever assembled. What a joy it is to come to work each day and see true energy, passion, and commitment. Never before have so many educators ever been brought together in such a positive way as to create the most amazing school. Thank you for creating magic for the students each and every day. I have to be better than my best self just to be on par with the excellence that you bring to our school. I'm in awe of all you do.

Dr. Brian Chinni, Dr. Paul Amoroso, and Dr. David Wiley are dear friends who I must thank for their never ending encouragement and friendship. They have all read far too much of my unpublished drivel – and yet still encourage me.

Tommy LoBue, you once said you learned leadership by standing on my shoulders. I don't know how that is possible. I was always standing on yours...

To John Fredericks and Dan Diljak, thank you for putting up with my daily discussions, thoughts, travails, and concerns. You've been rock

IMPOSSIBLE IS AN ILLUSION

solid friends from the first days we met at college. I have greatly enjoyed collaborating with both of you on my writing projects. Thank you for always lending a hand and being the truest of friends. I just wish you'd both move to New Jersey. Let's meet for lunch soon.

I always look forward to having pizza with Bob Dietz, a true inspiration…and a man whose knowledge of everything about life makes me realize how small I am and how much I don't know. I treasure our friendship.

I will always admire my dear friend Ed Hasse for being the very best of human beings. His kindness knows no bounds. He's seen me at my worst and is always forgiving. The only Ironman I know, I'll never be half the person or athlete that Ed is. I hope we can run together every day and in the NYC Marathon forever.

The list of great people who influence me on a daily basis is so long, but I'd be remiss not to thank and give my appreciation to Colin and Suse Bell, Mike Caulfield, Frank D'Amico, Andrew Del Mauro, Chris Nutland, Christine Lion-Bailey, Brian Winiarski, Michael Saffer…and so many others.

Thanks, of course, also to the wonderful Britta Eastburg Friesen, my outstanding editor. Thanks to author Rob Skead for all his encouragement. Thanks to Kitty Honeycutt at Ravenswood – I hope we achieve the great success we dream of together!

Of course, I must thank God, and Jesus, who are always by my side reminding me of what is good and right and teaching all of us what love truly is.

Which brings me back to my wife and kids – Laurie, Ryan, Alex, and Ethan – you are the loves of my life and my constant inspiration. You give me the motivation to be my best…for each of you. You make me realize that Impossible is an Illusion…because it is. I LOVE YOU!

The Weekly Memo

A Little Background to Begin…

IMPOSSIBLE IS AN ILLUSION

I became the principal of a highly successful middle school when I was just thirty years old. Some people thought I was too young to assume a position of such authority at such a young age. I didn't think so. I felt I was ready. I had been striving for that opportunity.

I had already been serving as high school vice principal following a successful (but relatively short) teaching career. From the start of my career as a teacher, I was placed in leadership positions and asked to sit on all sorts of committees. I had also earned a number of recognitions including the prestigious *A+ for Kids* Award and *Teacher of the Year* honors. At the time that I was appointed principal, I was enrolled (and working towards completing) a Doctorate in Education at Seton Hall University. I was also a member of the Executive Board (and would soon be President) of the New Jersey Middle School Association. All things pointed to me being ready for this next step in my leadership journey.

When people who didn't know me would come to my office for a meeting, the first thing many of them would say was, "You look awfully young to be a principal."

No one says that anymore when they meet me.

I'm not quite yet fifty, but I'm certainly no longer young. The other day a man saw me outside of my work environment and he said, "You look like a principal." That depressed me.

Besides old, haggard, worn-down, or tired, what does a principal look like? Me, I guess.

Sometimes, when I am most overwhelmed by life, I look in the mirror and see someone a lot older than me. The sad thing is that I don't see my father. I see my grandfather. I'm aging so fast that my reflection skipped a generation.

DR. PAUL SEMENDINGER

But it's all good.

When I assumed the position as Principal of Fieldstone Middle School in Montvale, New Jersey, I knew that I would have to find a way to communicate effectively with my staff. In the back of my mind, I thought a weekly bulletin might be a good way to accomplish this task. I had seen other school leaders use that approach. It seemed to be effective. In addition, my predecessor as principal had been doing just that. One way he would disseminate information was through a weekly notice that was written, printed, photocopied, and placed in each teacher's mailbox. (1998 was a long time ago. In those dark ages, we had not understood nor really embraced the Internet as a way to communicate.)

Since I enjoyed writing, I thought I might be able to make my newsletter a fun avenue to share motivation, inspiration, school news, and other pertinent facts.

In the beginning, I did not call this one-page newsletter *The Weekly Memo*; that actually came later. At the start, my written passages were all very short. The bulk of each issue focused primarily on school news and highlighted staff accomplishments. For fun, I did add my own touch by inserting certain "special features" such as "Facts of the Week," comics, educational jokes, trivia, and motivational quotes from famous people. After all, I wanted to keep the newsletter interesting. I needed the teachers to read it!

But throughout most of that first year, and even into my second and third years as principal, I did not introduce many of my own thoughts into that document outside of that document. I mostly stated simple facts, policies, procedures, and updates. The writer inside me was itching to get out, but I kept him contained at the start.

I'd always wanted to be a writer. I was published in my high school's literary journal, and I penned a series of short reflections in college. A fictional piece of mine was also published in my college's journal. People always told me I wrote well. Yet, as I tried to establish myself as a school leader, I was reluctant to showcase that side of my personality. In addition, feedback on the memos was positive. The teachers liked and were entertained by what they received each week. It's not always wise to alter a successful formula.

But, over time, I started to branch out. The newsletter became longer, and as I became more comfortable, I started to use the memo as a way to share my own perspectives and thoughts on a plethora of topics related to the school. Mostly, though, I used this bulletin as a way to inspire the teaching staff.

And it worked! Feedback was almost immediately positive. Many teachers started thanking me for writing passages that were uplifting. I was truly motivating them. I was told again and again that I wrote well. Some teachers even suggested that I publish a book. Imagine that?!

In those early days, I didn't write motivational passages each week. I branched out only sporadically. But through these exercises, I discovered something very interesting about myself; the more I wrote, the more I found I had to say. Rather than taxing my creative juices, writing made them flow more. I soon found myself writing about more and more topics. The bulletins became longer, and in a sense, I seemed to be creating more of a newspaper than a pamphlet. I gave this creation the unoriginal title, *The Weekly Memo.*

By now, my own thoughts had become the primary voice of *The Weekly Memo.* It was rare that I wouldn't find something in a school day, in my life, or in society, to write about. Most often, I wrote to inspire or motivate, but sometimes I just shared my thoughts and reflections. As I wrote, I found my own style, mostly following the standard rules of the English language, but sometimes inventing my own. Over the months and years of writing, I also set free my unique humor.

And people told me that I was funny.

Now, the last thing the world needed was for me to be encouraged like that!

Being a principal is a hard job. It is more difficult than most people can imagine. If one lets the position get to him, the role can be overwhelming. Principals can face untold amounts of negativity and criticism. And yet, I found as I wrote to inspire others, I also inspired myself. As I wrote to entertain others, I entertained myself.
Writing the memos helped me keep my focus as much as it helped the staff members keep theirs.

After about ten years in the middle school, I left my position to become an elementary school principal in a different district. This was one of the best professional decisions I ever made. While I loved my former school and district, my current school, Hawes Elementary School in Ridgewood, New Jersey, where I have served for the last ten years, is the most loving, caring, child-centered, and high-performing school that I have ever been part of. I like to call the work we do "magic" because we motivate, inspire, and energize children to be their very best. (To be fair, the school was very special before I came, but, in my own ways, I have certainly fostered and helped to maintain the wonderful atmosphere - or at least I haven't ruined it.)

When I assumed the elementary school principal position, I was already comfortable as a writer. *The Weekly Memo* was introduced immediately – again to positive reviews.

Over the years, *The Weekly Memo* has transitioned from a newsletter placed in mailboxes to digital formats accessed through the staff's on-line portals. Teachers can now read *The Weekly Memo* electronically anywhere around the world. Over time, I also branched out and began sharing my writing with others outside of the teaching staff. My newsletters to parents now contain reflective passages. I was encouraged to start a blog and I have placed some of my favorite writings there. Some of my passages have found their way to on-line forums including eduTopia and Linked-In. I now promote my writing on social media. Just recently, I have become a contributor to the popular Yankees blog, "*It's About The Money.*" It seems I'm writing a lot. For me, that's a good thing.

Over the last ten years, my writing style has changed a bit, but the messages have stayed pretty much the same. Each week I write about optimism, hope, hard work, fair play, kindness…and love. I reflect on my experiences in all areas and use humor as much as I can. (There's nothing like seeing other people laughing as they read my words; well, at least the words that were intended to be funny.)

The Weekly Memo has become part of who I am, and part of how I communicate and share my passion for life and my profession with my staff and now others around the world. *The Weekly Memo* has grown into something that inspires people – many of whom I have never met.

I write to inspire. I write to motivate. I write to remind others to work hard and to bring passion and commitment to everything they do. I write to remind people that life is good. And I write to hopefully bring cheer.

When I write, I often tell about parts of myself that I never really wanted to share. Writing humbles me. I have faced many of my own failures through my writings. When I write, I often see the mistakes I have made as a principal and even as a human being – even if these mistakes weren't so apparent at the time. Writing has helped me find the better parts of myself. I'm still working to be that better person.

DR. PAUL SEMENDINGER

The pages that follow contain are some of my favorite *Weekly Memo* passages from the last twenty years. I have, of course, revised and edited each passage, but the general themes and sentiments remain as they were originally printed. I have toned down some school specific themes to appeal to a larger audience. Education, though, plays a central role. I am, at heart, a principal. Maybe that's why people look at me and already know my profession.

I hope you can use this book to find inspiration. The passages can be read in any order. They can all stand alone. I hope you are motivated and entertained. I hope you laugh, at least a little. (Let me know which parts you found funny.)

Mostly, I hope my writings help each reader find the better parts of themselves. I believe in always striving. I believe in the goodness of all people. I believe we all have a great deal to share and to give.

I believe in laughter.

I believe in love.

I believe I can do anything. I believe we all can. But I also know that I am getting ahead of myself…

Impossible is an Illusion

◆

IMPOSSIBLE IS AN ILLUSION

I'm an optimist. I always believe that good will prevail. I look to the bright side. The glass is half full – even when it is half empty. I believe in miracles. Hope springs eternal.

I believe I can do anything. I believe we all can.

I have always thought like this. And in my lifetime I have been able to do some things that others (even myself at times) thought were impossible. Yet, they weren't. You see, Impossible is an Illusion. Nothing is impossible if you believe in yourself and if you work hard enough.

I've always wanted to be a published author. Writing is a hobby of mine and a way in which I express myself. I work diligently to improve my craft. Every day.

Now, since you're holding my book in your hands, you might be thinking, "Hey this guy accomplished his life dream." And I did. And that's pretty good! But I'm not finished. I still have other dreams, other hopes, and other goals to accomplish. And I have a lot more to write.

I believe we become successful when we determine to never set limits on ourselves. Too often we find reasons that we can't accomplish tasks rather than finding the will and the ways to do them.

I was never a runner. But, over time I decided that I should run a marathon. To accomplish this goal I bought running books and learned how to train to run 26.2 miles. Then, on a cold and damp Sunday in 2002, I ran the New York City Marathon. I accomplished a dream. I've now completed twenty marathons and I am looking forward to the next one. But, if you knew me as a kid growing up, you would have never thought that I would become an athlete. I loved sports and I played them, but I wasn't very good.

DR. PAUL SEMENDINGER

Growing up, I particularly loved baseball and had dreams of becoming a New York Yankee. I was certain I'd make it to the big leagues. I played baseball all the time. I went to a small high school where the good players reached varsity early on in their high school careers. I was certain that would help me...

Except, I never made varsity. My junior year, when most sophomores, all the juniors, and all the seniors were playing varsity baseball, I was pitching for the JV team. I was the only junior on the team. It was basically me and a bunch of freshmen.

Now, most people have cherished items from their high school sporting careers. I'm no exception. I have the game ball from the best game I ever pitched. Players typically save game balls when they throw no-hitters and such. My best game wasn't a no-hitter. It wasn't even close, it was a four hitter. That was the best I could do. I might be the only person in the world who has a baseball commemorating a four-hitter.

I lost more games than I won that year. That was the best season of my life.

I should also probably share that when I played sports as a kid, I was usually one of the last kids picked - for every game. It wasn't that I didn't try hard. It's because I really wasn't any good. I wanted to be an athlete, but the skills and my body didn't cooperate.

At the end of my elementary school experience, we had a yearbook that commemorated many of the students for their accomplishments, looks, or personalities. This was standard fare: Most Likely to Succeed, Cutest, Best Eyes, Most Athletic, Smartest...

Don't be misled. I was recognized in that yearbook. I was voted "Shortest."

IMPOSSIBLE IS AN ILLUSION

None of this is particularly inspiring.

In my life I have failed at a lot more than I care to admit. I fail at things all the time. If I'm good at anything, I'm good at failing.

Growing up, I wasn't even the most enthusiastic student. My grades were middling at best, until I went to college where I was inspired to actually use my brain.

Today I have a doctorate and am the principal of the greatest elementary school in the world – and that is no exaggeration. But, while I was plodding through middle and high school, even though I tried writing, I figured that I'd never really be a writer. I thought writers had to get straight A's.

Nonetheless, in order to achieve a dream, I started writing. I had written stories as a kid, but I started writing more seriously in high school. When I wrote, I wrote mostly for myself. I was writing a lot, but most often I was writing poorly. But it didn't matter because I was writing. I think I started to get better. I was even published in my high school's literary magazine. It was a start!

I wrote in college, even penned a few manuscripts (none publishable), but another story of mine was published in my college's literary journal. I was now two-for-two in getting published in small magazines that no one read.

As I settled into my profession, I kept writing. Much of what I wrote I kept to myself. But, I started sharing passages like these. People told me I was I pretty good. "You should get published," they'd say.

Eventually, I tried. I submitted my best works to literary agents and publishers. They all rejected everything I sent. I went to Writers' Conferences. At these conferences you can meet agents and publishers in person. (They charge extra for this, but I happily paid.)

They all rejected my works. I went to Writers' Retreats. These are more intimate settings where a writer can really spend time with agents and publishers. You have to pay a lot more money for these experiences. Those agents and publishers also rejected me. Every time. Some of the literary agents I met in those venues weren't particularly kind either.

It's not uplifting to travel hundreds of miles to spend hundreds of dollars only to be told you are an amateur and to be dismissed outright. These meetings are timed, and there were instances when I don't even think I got my full fifteen minutes with the professional. (Yes, I paid money to have a fifteen-minute conference with an agent who insulted me.)

I have faced a lot of rejection. Time and time again. Year after year. And yet, I'm now a published author. This might be the start of something big!

How can a non-athlete run a marathon? How can a non-academic child earn a doctorate and become a leader of a high performing school? How can a middling writer become a published author?

It's simple – I don't believe in the word *impossible*. I believe that I can do anything. I believe that any person can accomplish anything he or she sets out to do.

You see, Impossible is an Illusion.

We can do more than we think we can. We can achieve greater things than we ever thought possible. This happens when we allow ourselves to look beyond what we think is unachievable. This happens when we ignore the idea that certain things are impossible.

Unfortunately, the opposite is also true. When we put limits on ourselves, we set ourselves up to fail, or at least to not succeed.

IMPOSSIBLE IS AN ILLUSION

When we believe that there are things we can't do, it turns out that we can't do them.

Can't is a powerful word. The world is full of skeptics and people who will tell us what we can't do. When we believe others when they tell us what we can't accomplish, we lose. More, when we tell that to ourselves, we put the biggest limits on our potential. When this happens, things really do become impossible.

When we believe in impossible, life, in some ways, becomes easier. When tell ourselves that we can't do things, we don't have to do them. *Can't* allows us the necessary excuse to reject putting in the work necessary to accomplish great things.

Unfortunately, we often mistake *can't* for *can't* or, even worse, we use *can't* as an excuse so we don't have to attempt things that might be challenging.

"I can't quit smoking."

"I can't lose weight."

"I can't write."

"I can't paint."

"I can't play piano."

"I can't learn that."

We can be our own worst enemy, and in doing so, we make things impossible for ourselves.

Except, when we don't.

When we believe in ourselves, when we give our best efforts, when we try, when we work hard, when we are focused, we find that we CAN.

Impossible things are not really impossible. You just need to set your mind to doing whatever it takes in order to succeed.

We don't have to be defined by our failures. We don't have to be defined by the negative perceptions that others have of us. We don't have to be limited by the negative perceptions we have of ourselves.

Instead, we can do anything.

Impossible is an Illusion.

Kintsugi

IMPOSSIBLE IS AN ILLUSION

My son came home from college, and in a discussion with me brought up a Japanese word, kintsugi, that immediately opened up my mind to many thoughts.

It's wonderful to find new words, new ideas, and new ways of thinking.

And, just for the record, kintsugi is now my new favorite word.

* * * *

Let's walk through a scenario together.

You have a porcelain bowl on a shelf in your home. You love that bowl. It was given to you by your dear grandmother. One day, while dusting, you accidentally drop the bowl. It lands on the carpet and is not shattered, but it is broken into three uneven pieces. The breaks seem clean. If you repair them just right, you might not even be able to see the cracks.

You invest in the best repair tool possible. You may have found this item at a hardware store or purchased it from one of the many television commercials for products that repair items in seconds without any noticeable lines or blemishes. You work diligently and carefully. You think you did it. But, you didn't. Despite all your efforts, the cracks are still noticeable. Very noticeable.

You now have a few choices:

1. Put the bowl back on the shelf, even though it is now a flawed piece with visible defects.

2. Put the bowl in a cabinet. It is too precious to throw out, but you can't have a broken item on display.

3.   Throw the bowl away. "You can't keep everything," you say. Grandma would understand.

4.   Go back over the break in the bowl with a lacquer that makes the crack absolutely noticeable and then put the item back on display for all to see.

Which will you choose?

I would think most people would choose either #2 or #3. It would be rare for someone to choose #1. The final selection, #4, is unheard of.

* * * *

In America, we try to hide our mistakes. We cover them up. We run from them. Often times, even when confronted with them, we fail to admit them.

We make excuses.

We find scapegoats.

We justify.

We say, "It was just a misunderstanding."

Sometimes we even lie.

We do this because we do not like to face our flaws. We don't like admitting mistakes. We strive too hard to be perfect.

All of the time.

* * * *

IMPOSSIBLE IS AN ILLUSION

Kintsugi – (noun) *To repair with gold; The art of repairing with gold or silver lacquer and understanding that the original piece is more beautiful for having been broken.*

* * * *

With kintsugi, the mistake isn't run away from, the mistake is embraced. It is highlighted.

The spirit of kintsugi states that it is permissible to make a mistake with the understanding that mistakes are part of life and that we can learn and grow from them.

It's a whole different way of thinking.

It's a paradigm changer.

* * * *

Take a walk with me, please, into the home of a six year old child. Let's visit the child's bedroom. On a shelf are the more delicate items, maybe a special music box the child isn't allowed to touch. In the corner, in a large container are assorted stuffed animals. There is a very cute brown teddy bear in that bin that seems to have come right from the store. Now we look down on the floor. Lying on the floor is a stuffed bunny and a stuffed dog; we might name them Ears and Pup. Their special stuffed softness has been worn away. One can tell that these toys have spent more than their fair share of time in the spin cycle with the dirty clothes. The dog's nose is pushed in from being held closely night after night. The bunny seems to have once been torn on a seam and sewn back together.

Which of these items are the ones most loved by the child?

I dare say it isn't the music box or that cute bear in the bin.

DR. PAUL SEMENDINGER

* * * *

In America, we have a fascination with items in mint condition.

Old toys are worth more if they are in their original packaging. No one ever seems to ask about the fun of having a toy that is still in a box or plastic shell. Is it fun to have toys that one can't play with?

Baseball cards are now graded. Every flaw is detected and noticed. We even define different levels of perfection. A card in gem mint condition is much more desirable (and expensive) than a card that is just in mint condition. All of these cards are presented in thick plastic containers. The more valuable the card, the thicker the plastic. No one seems to ask if it is fun to have baseball cards embossed in hard plastic shells.

A valuable comic book is placed in a plastic sleeve and never exposed to sunlight. What good is a comic book that no one can see or read?

Cars by their very nature are left outside in the elements. Even cars that are garaged at night are exposed to rain and sun and snow and wind, to say nothing of shopping carts, stray balls, sticks, pot holes, suitcases, and the like. Yet, even with our cars, we have this ideal that they must be flawless and without any bumps, dents, or scratches.

We are obsessed with this goal of striving for perfection.

People today fill their garages and spare rooms with the original boxes (please don't damage the corners) from their "collectibles" in case those items ever need to be sold.

Some people even put their valuable possessions in storage units that they pay hundreds of dollars a year to maintain. They keep their best items away from their home, and in order to see them, they need to schedule a visit.

And then there is this idea of kintsugi... *"The original piece is more beautiful for having been broken."*

There is a big point here – we are more beautiful when we are not perfect. It is our flaws that give us our character.

It is in admitting and recognizing our flaws – and fixing them – that gives us our beauty.

* * * *

Imagine that broken porcelain bowl proudly on display with the cracks and blemishes very visible. What statement would that bowl make?

Imagine serving the guests you most wish to impress with plates that have chips and scratches.

Do you ever use your best china for breakfast? Why not?

Growing up, I enjoyed collecting baseball cards less when I cared more about their value than enjoying them just as cards. One can't constantly sort cards when they are sealed in plastic.

Kintsugi reminds us of what is truly valuable. When we consider kintsugi, we are able to differentiate between items of worth and items of value. When we consider kintsugi, we can understand and know what we truly cherish.

Some people say that items with blemishes have character. I agree. Each item tells a story. A pristine toy has no story to tell. On the other hand, those loved stuffed animals we met above, Ears and Pup, they tell stories about the child that cherishes them.

* * * *

If we are going to embrace failure as an essential part of learning, we have to also let our failures be noticed. We can't hide from them. We can't run from them. We can't make excuses when we err.

We need to be honest with ourselves. We need to be honest with our friends, our loved ones, our colleagues, and our clients.

It is of special note in my profession that some of the times when teachers and parents have understood me the best were when I began a difficult conversation with two simple words, "I'm sorry."

When we make a mistake, we need to recognize that mistake and find a way to grow from it. When we fix the mistake, we are practicing kintsugi.

More, when we embrace our mistakes, when we make them visible, and share them, and ask for help on how to correct them…that is true personal kintsugi.

When we stop trying to be perfect, we can discover where we need to grow. It is only then that we can begin to stop and repair the errors we make. But when we repair them, we must not do so in silence, but out in the open with transparency. You see, with kintsugi, there is one more important aspect.

The blemishes, the errors, the breaks are not just remedied; they are made visible with the most precious of materials – gold or silver.

IMPOSSIBLE IS AN ILLUSION

When we fix our mistakes, when we truly repair them, and we do so as to use our best resources as part of the process, then that is true kintsugi.

This is the critical aspect of kintsugi – in making the repair, we acknowledge that the piece (or in our case, the person) is more beautiful for having been broken.

Is This?

IMPOSSIBLE IS AN ILLUSION

I love baseball.

My dad loves baseball even more than I do.

That's where this story begins…and ends. It's what this story is all about. Baseball.

The Great American Game.

Well, maybe it's about more than that. It's about fathers and sons…and baseball.

* * * *

Sometimes, real life imitates art.

There was a movie that came out in the 1980's titled *Field of Dreams*. Ostensibly the movie is about a man who builds a baseball diamond in a cornfield in Iowa. He builds the field and numerous baseball greats arrive out from the growing corn to play ball on his magical sandlot. At one point, one of the players looks at the character who built the field and asks, "Is this Heaven?"

One of the greats to play on this field was the legendary and tarnished Shoeless Joe Jackson.

Shoeless Joe.

Joe Jackson was one of the greatest players to ever play professional baseball. In a thirteen year career, Jackson had a lifetime batting average of .356 which is higher than almost every other player in baseball history. This includes Ted Williams, Willie Mays, Mickey Mantle, Hank Aaron, Lou Gehrig, Joe DiMaggio, Stan Musial, and

Babe Ruth – yes, even Babe Ruth. None of them have a higher lifetime batting average than Shoeless Joe.

Joe Jackson's average is third all-time behind only Ty Cobb and Rogers Hornsby.

But Joe Jackson was caught up in the famous Black Sox scandal that involved fixing the 1919 World Series. He and seven of his teammates were found guilty, and thrown out of baseball for life. And death. "Permanently Ineligible" is what they call it.

Joe Jackson is not in the Hall-of-Fame. He's not eligible to get there. Even in death.

For the record, Joe Jackson died in 1951.

But *Field of Dreams* isn't really about Joe Jackson and his teammates getting a chance to play baseball again; it's about a man having a catch with his father. Even more, *Field of Dreams* is about the magic that exists when a father and his son make the time to play ball together.

* * * *

My mom and dad love to travel. Beginning in the late 1970's, when they purchased their first conversion van, a yellow 1978 Ford Econoline with a Turtle Top (you can't make this stuff up), they started driving to remote places across the United States.

Living in New Jersey is a great vantage point for traversing the country. Go west and the nation beckons!

In 1982, my parents, my sister and I headed off for the trip of a lifetime in that van – driving across the United States to California and back.

IMPOSSIBLE IS AN ILLUSION

In six weeks we covered over 10,000 miles, camping in the yellow van most of the time, with an occasional stop at a motel to "refresh."

The top of the van was called a Turtle Top because it popped up at night to provide an upper bunk for sleeping. In our sleeping bags, my sister and I shared the space upstairs. Mom and Dad slept downstairs on the double bed that folded up during the day into two rows of bench seats. It was called a conversion van for a reason – everything had a dual purpose.

We saw everything on that trip. Literally everything.

I remember a lot of canyons: The Black Canyon of the Gunnison, Bryce Canyon, Zion Canyon, and, of course, the Grand Canyon. There may have been others. We also saw a host of other great land formations – The Garden of the Gods, Mesa Verde, Devils Tower, Yellowstone, Yosemite, the Bad Lands, and the Great Salt Lake.

America is a great and amazing country.

And lest the reader think that it was all nature and no fun, yes, we also hit the tourist sites like the Corn Palace, Wall Drug, Las Vegas, Hollywood, Mount Rushmore, and, of course, Disneyland.
I could write pages about Disneyland. I love the Disney parks.

But, of all the places we visited along that great trip to California and back, my favorite stops were at the baseball stadiums.

I think these were my dad's favorites as well.

* * * *

Our first stop at a ballpark was in Kansas City. It was there that we had an opportunity to take a tour of the stadium and go, for the first time in my life, into the dugouts, on the field, and into the clubhouse.

While we were in the locker room, my mom noticed three discarded baseball bats, each with a crack. There were only three children in our tour group, so my mom asked if each of us could take a broken bat. Those days were before "game used equipment" was even a "thing" to collect. In an instant, the bats, otherwise heading to the garbage, were distributed to each child. I took Lloyd Moseby's bat. My sister was given a bat that had belonged to Wayne Nordhagen. The other kid, I am 100% certain of this, took Jesse Barfield's discarded bat – that was the one I wanted my sister to get. (I had been playing with Lloyd Moseby and Jesse Barfield in my Strat-o-Matic baseball league. They were both rookies who were doing very well.)

The previous night we had attended the game between the Kansas City Royals and the Toronto Blue Jays. The Royals won that game 5-4. George Brett had two hits and a run batted in. I still have the scorecard.

At the ballpark that night, my dad noticed Hank Bauer sitting in the stands. Hank Bauer had been a great Yankee outfielder in the 1950s and he was an important part of the Yankees teams that seemed to win the pennant every year. To that point, I had never heard of Hank Bauer, but my dad encouraged me to approach him and ask for his autograph – which I did. Hank Bauer smiled when I approached and later shook hands with my father. Hank Bauer, the legendary former Yankee, seemed like a kind and decent man.

I still have the autograph.

We also attended a baseball game in San Diego. The visiting team was the New York Mets. We thought it ironic that we traveled over 3,000 miles only to see a team from New York. I got numerous Mets players' autographs, something that probably wouldn't have happened at home, but what I recall the most is being put off by Dave Kingman. The great Dave Kingman refused to give me his signature.

IMPOSSIBLE IS AN ILLUSION

Maybe he refused because he was hitting only .221 at the time.

Back in those days my father taught me to keep score of every baseball game I attended, a tradition I carried well into adulthood. A number of years ago, after attending a plethora of Yankees games with my partial season ticket package, I lost track. I have a general list of every game I attended, but I'm not 100% certain it is accurate any longer.

My father taught me a lot, but most of all, he taught me to love baseball.

* * * *

In subsequent years, following our epic family trip to California, my sister and I, of course, grew up, went to college, found jobs, created our own lives, and began families of our own.

Mom and Dad continued to travel whenever they could. And, whenever they found themselves near Iowa, they'd visit the Field of Dreams.

For my father, it was a place of magic. He likes to recount how real life picks up right where the movie ends, with cars lined up to visit the field – a place where friends and families can gather to play ball, if only for a short while.

My dad has shared many stories of his visits to the Field of Dreams. He tells of the families he met there and of the time he loaned his Louisville Slugger to an anonymous person so he could "bat some out."

My dad always threw off the mound there to his favorite catcher, my mom. He was still trying to perfect, even in his seventies, his signature knuckleball.

Amid corn stalks, clay, and grass, my father still lives his dream of reaching the Major Leagues.

"Now pitching for the Red Sox, the game's oldest rookie, number 21..."

There was only one thing missing from all these memories.

Me.

His one and only son.

* * * *

For many years I entertained dreams of surprising my dad with a trip to Iowa to play on the Field of Dreams. I thought it would be a great thing to do.

I thought it was something I *should* do.

And yet, it never happened.

* * * *

I have three wonderful boys. My focus on raising them, and being an active presence in their lives – in every way – left me with precious little time to run off to Iowa with my own father to play baseball.

Iowa isn't exactly right around the corner.

It wasn't for a lack of wanting, but life gets in the way. My quest to be a great dad to my children left me incapable of always being a great son. Sure, I have always made time for my parents, but I didn't have days upon days to go to Iowa to play ball.

IMPOSSIBLE IS AN ILLUSION

As nice of an idea as that was, it just didn't happen.

Years ago, my dad and I started a tradition of always having a catch on Father's Day. I love this. In a way, we have made our own field of dreams in our backyards.

And that, I reasoned, was the closest we'd ever get to the real thing.

Or so I thought.

* * * *

We all grow up. In 2015, my oldest son was at Lafayette College. My middle son was at Williams College. My youngest was completing his sophomore year of high school…

No longer did my kids seem to need me on a daily basis.

For the first time, maybe in my "forever," I seemed to be getting some free time.

On one occasion, as my father shared another story of his experiences at the Field of Dreams, I thought to myself, "*I really must get there with him.*"

* * * *

As a young dad, I couldn't really see beyond my own kids and my own daily needs. For many years, I was way over extended. I was working as a principal, teaching as an adjunct college professor, coaching numerous sports teams, helping with the Boy Scouts, volunteering at church, serving as a mentor to future school administrators, playing in an "old-man" softball league, and trying to make time for my own family's experiences by traveling with them to great places – including, of course, ballparks.

I don't regret any of that. I loved every minute. But I didn't afford myself much free time. The only time I gave to myself was spent running as I picked up this crazy habit of competing in marathons.

Now, with my children growing, and a very understanding wife, I started to think that going all the way to Iowa to have a catch with my dad wasn't all that crazy.

I also started to consider alternatives to driving there. Maybe I could fly to Iowa, and meet my parents out there. I knew they'd want to drive. They always want to drive.

The idea began to blossom.

* * * *

I have a great relationship with my mom and dad. They've always been there for me. We live only two miles apart and we get together most weeks for what we call "Pizza Thursday."

But, all that being said, I felt there was a chance that my dad might not like the idea of meeting in Iowa after all these years to go to the Field of Dreams. Maybe he had other plans. Maybe he moved on.

As silly as it sounds, I didn't want to get rejected from my father, so, while I had the idea, and was quite certain it was a good idea, I didn't bring it up.

I get a lot of good ideas in my head that I just don't bring up.

* * * *

And then it happened, late August 2015.

Life as we knew it changed.

IMPOSSIBLE IS AN ILLUSION

Dramatically.

In an instant I saw that my parents were all too mortal, and that they were every bit of their age. The call came in the late evening. It was my mom. "Dad is having trouble breathing, don't worry, but I want you to know we're going to the hospital. I called the ambulance."

I rushed to my parents' house and arrived just after the ambulance. The paramedics were already inside the house.

My father had had health scares before. But this, somehow, seemed different.

Dad couldn't breathe.

* * * *

At the hospital, they tried everything, but dad still gasped and struggled for breath. The Emergency Room was all a buzz. I saw concern on people's faces.

Worse, I saw fear in my father's eyes. I'm certain he thought he was dying.

I had never before seen fear in my father's eyes.

He couldn't breathe; he struggled, constantly, for air.

It was at this point that the doctor examining my father said the words that resonate with us still today. "I have to trach him."

Discussions followed, but we were told that time was of the essence. While I remained calm and level-headed, there was a stronger person in the room – my mother. She took in all the information. She called friends and asked for prayers. She remained by my father's side.

When she heard the word "tracheotomy," she immediately thought of my father's friend who had a trach many years ago.

"He and dad still communicate," she said. "We can get through this."

My sister, a nurse, arrived. She confirmed the decision: the tracheotomy was the only answer for this immediate crisis.

* * * *

My father never smoked. He exercises regularly. He doesn't drink. When I tell people that he had a tracheotomy, or in other words that he now breathes through a hole they cut in his neck to his windpipe, they assume he was a smoker. It just isn't true.

The best that any doctor can explain is that this was simply a freak virus.

"Sometimes it happens."

People still ask, "Why did your dad need a trach?"

The simple answer is because he couldn't breathe.

* * * *

There was emptiness when I sat with my father in the hospital room the next day. I had taken my mom home to rest and I was now alone with my dad. All things considered, his spirits were good, but he was no longer the same man.

My dad couldn't talk.

As we sat in the hospital room, in silence, I wished to hear my father's voice just one more time.

IMPOSSIBLE IS AN ILLUSION

He tried to mouth words to me, but I am not good at lip reading.

Instead, I had a pad of paper, and we started to write to each other.

We talked, a little, about the hospital, but mostly, we talked about baseball. Dad loves the Red Sox. We spent a lot of time writing down Red Sox line-ups on pieces of paper.

Jerry Remy, Dwight Evans, Jim Rice, Carl Yastrzemski, Tony Perez…

Rico Petrocelli, Jim Longborg, Tony Conigliaro…

Vern Stephens, Bobby Doerr, Joe Cronin, Dominic DiMaggio, Mel Parnell… and Ted Williams.

My dad loved Ted Williams.

Still does.

Ted Williams was born on August 30. I know that date very well. It's also my mom's birthday.

Teddy Ballgame was born in 1918. That was 21 years before my mom.

* * * *

It's cliché, but baseball gave my dad and I something to talk about when there weren't words for anything else.

The other thoughts were too scary.

Would he ever talk again? Would he be able to eat? What would his new life look like?

Baseball was safe. It was common ground. Constant. Unemotional. We could name players for hours. And we probably did.

Dad wrote the names down. I talked. It was silly for me to write.

Dad could still hear.

* * * *

There was a miracle while my dad was in the hospital. He learned how to talk again. The medical experts couldn't explain it.

My dad can now talk, not quite like before, but pretty darn close.

* * * *

After a few weeks of being home, the doctors said that my dad could resume all life activities. "Including travel?" my dad asked.

"Yes, including travel," came the reply.

This time I wasn't going to put off this crazy thought of mine. I didn't quite say it in so many words, but the spirit of what I asked was the same…

"Hey, Dad, wanna have a catch?"

* * * *

One of my favorite activities in the world is just having a catch. I love to throw a ball to a partner.

My father taught me how to throw and catch. We played ball a lot when I was a kid.

IMPOSSIBLE IS AN ILLUSION

I taught my sons to play ball. We still try to make the time to get our gloves out and chuck.

There's nothing like it.

I try to remember to savor every one of these experiences.

I have been waiting for many months now in eager anticipation of what will be the most memorable catch of my life. Mom and Dad are already on the road and heading for Iowa.

In a few short days, I'll be flying there.

To have a catch.

With my dad.

I Am A Reader

◈

IMPOSSIBLE IS AN ILLUSION

*T*his might have to be filed under "ridiculous," but it's a true story, and I think it's a good story.

I sometimes like to be a tour guide. I was able to find an outlet for that part of my personality by running historical trips for our local Boy Scout Troop. All three of my sons were active Boy Scouts (and they all worked hard to achieve the rank of Eagle Scout). I found that this was one way that I could give back to the troop. As a former history teacher, I greatly enjoy venturing to historical sites to share my passion for history with others. In my years with the Boy Scouts, I led tours of Gettysburg, Valley Forge, Washington's Crossing, Philadelphia, Central Park, and more.

One year, I provided the Wyckoff Boy Scouts with an extensive three-day tour of Washington, D.C. As we explored many of the great sites in our nation's capital, I was inspired by the many people who were jogging, seemingly everywhere. Washington seemed to be a city filled with runners. I said to my son Alex, who was fifteen at the time, "I have been in Washington, D.C. forty million times, but never to just have fun. It seems every time I'm here I am running or planning trip of some sort. I would love to run around the monuments. Wouldn't it be great to just come here and run?" To my surprise, Alex replied, "Yes." We immediately decided to return to DC the next summer to explore the city in our running shoes.

True to our word, Alex and I did just that. We woke up early one day and made the five-hour drive to Washington, D.C. We were there well before noon and quickly prepared for our running adventure.

What an experience! We ran around every possible monument going from the Abraham Lincoln Memorial to the Capitol. We also ran around the Tidal Basin (and saw the Martin Luther King Memorial before it even opened). It was awesome. Since we planned to run again the next day (if once is fun, then two times must be doubly as much fun), I had arranged for a hotel stay.

After we finished our run, we showered, had lunch, and toured the city on foot and Metro.

Alex requested that we visit the Library of Congress since we did not tour that location on the Boy Scout trip. As such, we set out to visit America's most famous library. Alex, who is a huge reader, loved it.

But for those who have never been, when you visit the Library of Congress, you don't really visit the library part. Instead, visitors enter a library museum. Regular visitors do not get up close and personal with the collection of books, although they are allowed to look out behind a soundproof glass wall at the people who are permitted to read and research there.

As we gazed at the fortunate readers who were actually in the library, Alex told me that he wished we could go into that reading room…

Well, one of the best parts of being a Dad is being able to work miracles (and the older my kids get, the harder this is to do), so I figured I'd try to get us into the actual library.

I approached a security guard and asked, "How does one get to use the reading room?"

The guard replied, "You need a Library of Congress Library Card."

We, of course, didn't have such a thing. We didn't know how to get one, and being just regular tourists, it didn't seem like we'd have much chance of acquiring such a card, but, I figured I'd ask anyway…

"How does one get a Library of Congress Library Card?" I inquired.

IMPOSSIBLE IS AN ILLUSION

The guard looked at me and then replied in a matter-of-fact manner, "You go outside, cross the street, and go to Room 140 in the Madison Building. It's a multi-step process; they don't just give them out. You need to be a researcher."

I turned to Alex and said, "Let's get some library cards!"

We ventured over to the Madison Building and went through the process. Just as the guard had stated, there were a number of steps; they don't just give the cards away. In order to get a card you need to prove that you are a researcher and that you'll put the card to good use. The keepers of the library ask some pointed questions, but we got through it. You see, I had an ace in the hole.

My great-great grandfather was an early inventor of the camera. Not many people have heard of August Semmendinger, but I have (of course). I am also the world's leading expert on the history of the Semmendinger Camera. (This is a title that I have given myself.) I used my sincere desire to research my family's history as the rationale for acquiring a Library of Congress library card. It's all true, and it worked!

Sadly, because Alex was fifteen, he was not old enough to get a card of his own. Still, he was permitted to tag along with me.

With the library card in hand, Alex and I ventured over to the Library of Congress and were permitted inside. We felt like we had access to some exclusive club and, in a sense, we did. We found secret reading rooms and displays which were not open to the public. There was even a room for children that contained all sorts of treasures including Harry Potter books from around the world. We of course ventured into the library itself and perused the racks and racks of books. At one point, we looked up to see the museum visitors, on the other side of the glass, looking down at us!

After about an hour in the library, we decided to leave. There's a lot to see in Washington, D.C. and we resolved that we'd be back to research in earnest and experience more of what the Library of Congress has to offer. We also knew that we'd have to go back so Alex could acquire a card of his own.

And the story could end there, but it doesn't because as I looked at the library card that has my likeness stamped on its front, I noticed something very interesting...

The library card gives me a title. I'm not sure of the other titles the Library of Congress stamps on the cards, but mine labels me as a READER. That's my title. The card is even verified. I find this to be extremely interesting.

I have an official document from the United States Government, a Library of Congress library card, that labels me as a reader.

I think this is very cool.

I'm not a patron. I'm not a client or a subscriber. I'm not a constituent or a member. I'm not a researcher. They don't call me an investigator or an examiner. I'm not a sage, a philosopher, or a theorist. They don't call me a wise man or even learned.

But they do call me a reader.

And that's really the point of this piece.

Sometimes we live by the titles we've earned. Sometimes we live by the titles we're given.

As silly as it might be, I'm proud of this card. I like that I have a card that identifies me as a reader.

IMPOSSIBLE IS AN ILLUSION

It's a title that was bestowed upon me by the very nature of the card, but it's also one I believe I have earned. After all, one doesn't seek to acquire a Library of Congress library card unless one reads. Believe it or not, I don't think I would have wanted any other title. I'm not sure if I'm wise or if I am a researcher, but I am a reader. The title fits me.

When we give titles to others, we are bestowing upon them certain attributes: friend, child, parent, colleague, confidant, lover, and spouse. All of those words have connotations and expectations. When we label, we often legitimize. When we label, we often verify.

It can be hard to shake a label once it is given. Or earned.

As such, we should be careful when we throw out epithets, for in society, we often call people things which they are not. This can have hurtful consequences. This happens across professions, on all sides of politics, and in countless other areas as well.

We should also strive to wear the labels that most characterize ourselves. I hope to wear titles like "UNDERSTANDING" and "KIND." It's nice when people tell me that I am those things.

The world I know best is the world of education. In my profession I can see the power of words and titles. I often see how positive titles can transform and truly validate and inspire a child. I know how great it is to be called a reader.

This is what happens in elementary classrooms each and every day – teachers confer on their students the title of READER. When a child is identified as a reader, he or she always feels proud. Being a reader truly is something special. The world opens up when one learns that he or she can make sense of all the writing everywhere. Once one knows how to read, the world holds no more secrets. A reader can find out and learn about anything!

This is the type of magic that teachers deliver in classrooms on a daily basis. They give titles: Reader. Mathematician. Scientist. Artist. Musician. Athlete. Caring Person. Friend. These titles are like keys that open all of the doors of learning.

It is how learners are created.

Conversely, it is equally as important to be very careful when we assign titles to children such as Lazy, Liar, or Bully. Do we want our children to live up to the labels that the adults in the world assign to them often for behaviors that children aren't even cognizant of. (I know a certain high-energy author who wasn't the most motivated student in school. I hate to imagine what I'd be today if I believed that I was inherently lazy or disinterested.)

We must make the effort and take the time to notice and value the good we see. When we do this, we can encourage others. We can build them up. When we give others positive titles, they most often live up to those lofty expectations.

This is true of children, absolutely, but it's also true for all of us. Call a person kind, and see what they can do. Most often they actualize the word through continued kindness. When we share love, we create love.

I know that I believe most of the titles that are given to me. I work hard to maintain the positive impressions that others have of me. It's part of who I am and who I desire to be.

I want to be so many things, but for now I'll just focus on one. I am a reader. And if you don't believe me, I have the card to prove it.

IMPOSSIBLE IS AN ILLUSION

*A S*ense of *W*onder

◆

IMPOSSIBLE IS AN ILLUSION

I recently came across a passage that suggested that we should always "maintain a sense of wonder" in our lives. I love the idea of seeking wonder, or magic, in the mundane.

Life isn't always about the things we have to do, and even when it is, that doesn't preclude us from seeking the good and something special in every situation. This is important to recognize and acknowledge because there can be good everywhere and at any time. It's simply about maintaining that sense of wonder.

I think that we often rush through our lives. We get so busy shuffling ourselves and our kids back and forth to so many activities and events that we often don't stop to appreciate each of these experiences. We get so caught up in all the moving that we really don't even consider what it is that we are going to and where we are leaving from. All we know is that we're rushing and there is something more to do.

As I consider this, I'm not advocating doing less. That's not in my nature or character. I can't do less. (In fact, I'm always trying to do more.) But, I am suggesting that we add an element of attentiveness to the activities that we are participating in because when we do this, each one becomes more meaningful.

Maintaining a sense of wonder (or looking for good in the mundane) isn't easy to do:

– It isn't easy to find the good as your kid is playing right field and also striking out three times on a forty-two-degree day in early April.

– It isn't easy to do when your child is struggling through word problems with a tutor.

– It isn't easy to do when you are at one location and know you need to be somewhere else.

– And it isn't easy to do when you have a collection of obligations and responsibilities that are all screaming for your attention.

But I am saying that we should try, because there is always another perspective:

– That child playing right field is part of a team. That is something special. She wears a uniform (or a t-shirt) that signifies that she is on that team. That is also something special. There is something good and valuable and wonderful about being on a team. And, while it might seem that teams and games will be part of your child's life (and your lives) forever, they won't be. Our children grow up fast. The games end - far too quickly.

– There's also something special about struggling through any endeavor, even word problems. In the example above, watching a child struggle can be frustrating for a parent. But it is that very struggle that teaches the child such important life skills as perseverance and tenacity. And, when the child finally succeeds; there is magic in that. That's learning. Throughout that child's life there will always be struggles and things he has to work through in order to understand. There is good there. When we take the time to maintain a sense of wonder, we remember, recognize, and find the good, even in the struggles.

– As for the other obligations that are all screaming for our attention, the sad truth is, most often, they can wait. The text, the phone call, the e-mail…they can all wait. There is a benefit to this. If we rid ourselves of unnecessary distractions, it allows us the space and time to maintain the sense of wonder in our lives and in our children's lives.

And, when it comes to our children especially, there is so much wonder there, that our focus should always be on capturing it, gathering it, and cherishing all of it in our hearts!

IMPOSSIBLE IS AN ILLUSION

Always.

Where will you find the wonder today?

Crash-Test Teaching

IMPOSSIBLE IS AN ILLUSION

Last fall, as my son Ethan and I were having some fun watching football, I was struck by a commercial that showed a car going through crash tests. It seemed to be typical commercial, similar to the ones we have all seen thousands of times. But this commercial was different. The subject seemed less about the car and more about the engineer who ran the crash test. In this ad, the engineer carefully positioned each crash test dummy in the car. He took great care with each. The viewer is struck by the empathy that this worker has for these inanimate objects. And then we see that the dummies are dressed and designed to actually look like real people. It quickly becomes apparent that the reason the engineer showing such care is because he is imagining that the dummies are his own wife and children. He then puts himself in the driver's seat.

As the commercial rolls to its finish, with the car crashing, the screen turns black and a voice says, "When you don't think of them as dummies, something amazing happens."

It was an extremely powerful commercial – one that struck and resonated within my heart.

What makes the commercial so powerful is that it is true, not just for cars and crash dummies, but for everyone. Always. This is especially true in my job where we deal with children.

When I think about that commercial, a few important perspectives come to mind.

First, when we stop to consider that the children who come to our classrooms every day are more than just faces, we are able to see beyond ourselves. One aspect of all great educators is that they know that their job is something more than just an occupation. Great teachers know that their actions matter. They know that their approach matters. They know that their daily decisions matter. Most of all, great teachers know that their students matter. Because of all of this, great teachers are selfless.

Second, when we think of our students as unique individuals, with all the curiosity and wonder and discovery that comes with that, something amazing also happens – we end up caring even more. There is something magical about childhood that we are fortunate to be part of. Because of this, we have the opportunity to enrich children's lives in so many ways. When we create lessons that excite children, we are creating magic. When we value children and respect them, we are teaching them that they matter – because they do.

Third, when we do these things, and when give of ourselves for our students, we enrich not only them, but ourselves. Teaching is a unique occupation in that we get to see the rewards of our efforts on a daily basis. Children's smiles come out when they feel safe, respected, appreciated, and loved. It becomes a reciprocal arrangement – our great work leads to happy children who, in turn, return our appreciation through their own kindness. Is there anything as wonderful as being on the receiving end of an enthusiastic smile from a child?

Fourth, there are times when we can get frustrated with our students. It happens, even to the very best teachers. There will be times when a child doesn't do the right thing or shows little growth or no improvement. Still, that child needs our support. When teachers take ownership for each child in their class, they find it easier to give each child the supports he or she needs.

Fifth, a literal translation of the commercial reminds us that even the "slowest" or most challenged student isn't a "dummy" – he is a very real person. We should never put labels on kids – especially negative ones. Those crash test mannequins aren't "dummies" to the worker. That's why he does his best work – to save lives. If you think of it in a certain way, teachers also save lives. Teachers establish an environment that protects children. Great teachers always remember to help each child grow, not just academically, but socially and emotionally, as well. When teachers teach to the whole child, they open up the lives of their students to unlimited potential.

Finally, I think the most powerful aspect of this commercial isn't the words, but what is going on in the man's head. He doesn't see the crash dummies as mere objects, but as his own family. As I watched, I thought, "He's putting his own family in the car – and then himself. Wow! What a powerful message about his level of commitment." This was the big moment of the commercial.

As teachers, when we treat every child as if he or she were our own, we invest even more into how we act, how we plan, what we say, and what we do.

When we think about our actions in this light, it can make us think and do things differently. It can make us do things better. The philosophy of giving beyond ourselves can give us the patience we need when a child exhibits frustrating behaviors. It can make us take that extra moment to personalize our messages. When we think of our students as our own, we make the extra efforts to invest ourselves in them. When we do these things, we also find ourselves giving our students the unconditional love they all deserve.

The technician in the commercial exhibits so much faith in the car that he is testing that he's willing to put his family inside. As great educators, we should always teach as if the people we care the most about are the ones we are instructing. We need to always remember to put our own children and our own loved ones (at least figuratively) in our classrooms. Our classrooms should be safe places for our students so that they are protected from the crashes that will inevitably come before them.

When we invest at this level, we know we are doing the right things for children.

No Message – Just Enjoy!

◆

IMPOSSIBLE IS AN ILLUSION

*T*his story happened during a class visit.

A first grade teacher and a student were looking at an early reader book that discussed going grocery shopping. It was a very simple book that followed a pattern designed to help emerging readers. On the left page was short text. On the right page was a picture describing the text. A sample looked like this:

The student turned to a page showing a basket of tomatoes. She read, "I buy potatoes."

The teacher complimented the student for sounding out the word, but encouraged her to now use the correct beginning letter.

"Look at the starting letter. It's a T. Try again."

"I buy potatoes."

"What does T sound like?"

"I buy potatoes."

"T - t, t, t. Try again."

"I buy potatoes."

"Good try. Let's look at the picture. Those are not potatoes. The word sounds like potatoes, but it starts with T."

"I buy potatoes."

"What is pictured there in the bag? The red items, you might find them on a salad."

"I don't know."

"Those are tomatoes, dear. T, T, tomatoes."

The student was then encouraged to read on. She read two more pages when she came to a page with a picture of potatoes. The teacher was still reading with the student.

"Oh look," the teacher said. "As we prepare to read this, let's remember to look at the beginning letter of the word."

"P."

"Correct. Good job! Please read the sentence."

"I buy pears."

All They Do Is Win

◆

IMPOSSIBLE IS AN ILLUSION

*T*he date was November 20, 2016. It was the first bitterly cold day of autumn - a sure sign that winter was on the horizon. My wife Laurie and I sat in the cold stands of Kean University with a large collection of fans, mostly parents, watching the Ramapo High School Boys' Soccer Team play their final game of the season in their quest to win the New Jersey State Championship.

It had been a largely successful season for this varsity soccer team. Going into this final match, they were undefeated. More than that, they hadn't even tied any games. Along the way, the Ramapo Boys had won the League Championship, the Bergen County Championship, and the State Sectional Championship. In this processional of dominance, they outscored their opponents by a total score of 74-7. They had never allowed more than one goal a game.

To further illustrate the strength of this team, they came into the championship game ranked as one of the top twelve high school teams in the entire nation. Yes, across the United States of America. This collection of players was a powerhouse.

All they did was win…

What happened in that championship game is of little significance to this essay because, surprisingly, I am not writing just about great soccer or winning. Rather, this passage is about a program that was (and is) successful. More, it's about a program that, believe it or not, is not really about winning.

I know all of this because I saw this team up close in a number of ways. If I didn't quite have a front row seat, I was pretty close. My son Ethan was a contributing member of this outstanding soccer squad.

Ethan was a mid-fielder. As a man who coached Ethan throughout his entire soccer career (in recreational leagues, not at a highly competitive level), I know a bit about Ethan's soccer ability; after all, I'm also his dad. I have seen Ethan meet his fair share of success on the soccer pitch. It was always a special honor to be his father, his fan, and his coach. For Ethan's recreational soccer experience, I absolutely had a front row seat; in fact, I often drove the (proverbial) bus. It was quite a wonderful ride.

The remarkable thing about the Ramapo High School soccer team is, that for as successful as it has been, winning is not the ultimate objective. In fact, in team discussions, championships, undefeated seasons, or even wins, are not the focus. Winning isn't the defining characteristic of success for this team.

You see, the great coach, Evan Baumgarten, has built something more than a team. In his over thirty years at the helm, he has developed a program. There is a big difference between a team and a program. A program comes from a philosophy that spans a long period of time. A team is just a collection of players at a particular moment. Successful teams are notable. Successful programs are harder to create, more difficult to sustain, and are much more impressive than any single winning club.

This soccer program is one that cares more about the boys as people, not necessarily soccer players, than the end result of the games. Values such as teamwork, character, determination, focus, fair play, and yes, even kindness define this program. Winning comes next, only after those primary objectives are met.

This focus begins before the kids ever set foot on the soccer field. This philosophy begins before the players even reach high school.

I need to take a step backwards, for a brief moment. I have seen this program for close to a decade because Ethan's older brother, Ryan, was a defender on Ramapo's last State Championship team. As a man who was pretty involved in soccer for a long time – yes, I was also Ryan's soccer coach throughout his childhood soccer experiences – I knew that what was taking place with this year's team was no different than what had been taking place for a long time.

Before ever becoming part of the program, prospective players are invited to a soccer meeting toward the close of their eighth grade experience. Coach Baum (as he is known) runs this mandatory meeting. It is here that the coach outlines his expectations for the players and their parents. This is how one builds a program, and not just a team. All interested parties must understand the philosophy and the expectations from the start. I have been to many of these meetings and I don't recall winning ever being the topic of discussion. Instead Coach talks about teamwork, dedication, perseverance, and…school work. The players, and their parents, are told that, for these teams at least, academics comes first.

And yet, all they do is win.

The soccer experience begins in earnest when the school year comes to a close as the boys participate in a competition for teams across the nearby counties. This tournament is run just for fun. There are no winners or losers. No one is declared a champion. Rather, the tournament is an opportunity for teams to come together just to play soccer. The kids play and parents assist by running snack stands and serving as field managers. The event takes place over a June weekend. Afterwards summer beckons.

Over the summer, the boys are invited to informal pick-up games that take place during an "open soccer" program. These games are attended by current players, future hopefuls, and even returning athletes from college and beyond. If individual coaches are present, they don't run the games. Instead, "Open Soccer" is run by kids. If one desires to build a program, this is a great way to start. I am convinced that my ninth grade self would have been delighted in engaging and sharing a soccer field with past championship players. I think it would have brought out the best in me.

In mid-August, the official season begins with tryouts. After only two or three days, the players are informed if they made the various teams. I know in our family we waited with great anticipation each year hoping that our sons would be chosen for the various teams from Freshman, through Junior Varsity (JV) to Varsity. They did! For each of Ryan's and Ethan's four years at high school, they made a team that was part of this championship tradition.

But here is where I must also be a bit more honest. Neither Ryan nor Ethan played club soccer growing up. Neither was an elite player. They were good, they had talent, but they weren't groomed to be varsity athletes. Prior to high school, each boy's soccer experiences were at the lowest competitive level – recreation. Their coach, who also happened to be their dad, wasn't the greatest soccer mind. Our soccer teams had fun, we won a few games, but I could only take them so far. I am no soccer expert.

As such, both boys were long shots to make the team each year, especially their senior years when they'd be striving for the varsity squad. And here is another of the character traits and philosophies of Coach Baumgarten that seems counter-intuitive to building a winning program – except in rare circumstances, if the players are kind, hard working, polite, and "good kids" in general, he doesn't often cut them.

That's how my sons made the teams.

And here, again, is where Coach Baum is so much different from other coaches - he meets with each player each year. He outlines his expectations of them. He gave both of my sons the same message: "You're a good person. I want you on the team. But, you have to realize, you won't play very often. There are better players who will play ahead of you." Rather than creating a squad of players who might be disgruntled at their lack of playing time in the games (to be sure, every player is expected to give his best at every practice), the players on Ramapo's squad know their roles exactly. My sons signed onto this without any hesitation.

Once the players make the team, they are showered with a collection of gear, most of which they get to keep - forever. They get shirts, hats, shorts, and socks. Most often they also receive coats, scarves, beanies, and sometimes even duffle bags. It's a treasure trove of soccer paraphernalia – and, for the players it's all free. Every player at all the levels gets these items – and they all receive the same items. This demonstrates that they all are part of the bigger program. In addition, the shirts each year have a motivational slogan that remind all the players that they are part of something special and something bigger than themselves.

The year my son Ethan went to the State Championship, the slogan read, *"The more we give of ourselves to see others succeed, the greater our value to the team."*

It is a clear message, and while the slogan differs from year to year, the overriding message is the same. It's about working together; it's about the team. It's not about winning.

And yet…all they do is win.

In the pre-season, the varsity squad practices daily, but they do more than just drill. They travel together, they eat together, they have bonding experiences, they work together and they become more than a collection of players. They become a team.

One of the experiences they go through is called "27 Hours." It is what it seems – 27 hours of exercise, drills, and bonding. This is both not as bad as it seems and worse. This year, part of the experience took place at West Point at the U.S. Military Academy. West Point graduates - military officers in other words - helped with this training. It's grueling, but the boys love it. After experiencing 27 Hours, they feel, more than ever, a special camaraderie. The winning that comes later grows out of this bond.

Throughout the season, as the games come, practices are also a constant. Yet, Coach's words ring true. Players miss practice in order to get extra help in their classes or to study. Seniors (and some juniors) also miss to visit colleges or to participate in other important obligations.

During this past season, Ethan had to reach out to Coach Baumgarten to ask permission to miss a practice and a team barbeque because it was the day he was being honored for attaining his Eagle Scout Award. Of course, Coach Baum was more than understanding.

In fact, Coach was so proud of Ethan, he came up with a special way to show it.

As Ethan prepared for his Eagle Scout Court of Honor, greeting leaders, fellow scouts, family members, and dignitaries, the entire varsity team, including the coaching staff, was gathering outside in the parking lot. Now, at least where we live, the Boy Scouts are not considered cool. Soccer, yes; scouts, no. And yet, they all came, in their soccer uniforms, one by one in a straight line… the entire squad, to attend, honor, and celebrate their teammate, who also happened to be the last kid off the bench.

That's how a program is made. All players are valued, from the first to the last. And that's a big reason why all they do is win.

This caring attitude begins right at the start. During Ethan's freshman year, he was getting frustrated. He was coming back from an appendectomy. His play suffered as did his playing time. High school was proving to be a challenging step. His older brother Ryan was away at college. Life had changed – a lot. One evening, as my wife and I were folding laundry, the doorbell rang. Standing outside was Ethan's freshman soccer coach, Coach Yaz.

Doctors today don't make house calls, but great coaches and great people do. Coach came by just to check up on his player and to talk to his caring parents. When does that happen? Coach Yaz stayed for a good thirty minutes. He echoed the same sentiments discussed throughout this essay. He also talked about God. You see, faith also plays a role in all of this – even in the secular sports world.

As the current season progressed I occasionally asked Ethan what Coach Baum said during his pre-game and half-time meetings with the team. Ethan pondered for a moment and said, "He just tells us to be good people. That's what it's all about. In addition, Coach also turns the meetings over to the kids." Imagine that! At these most critical competitive times, the players, high school kids, do most of the talking, strategizing, and motivating.

On another occasion, I asked Ethan what drills his coaches run the team through. I wondered if he did things a lot differently than I had. Ethan's response shocked me. "Dad, it's about the same. We're just at a higher level now. It's all about effort and just being our best." I probed further. "What strategy does he teach?"

"Work together, be a team. It's that simple, Dad."

And there we were, Laurie and I, and all the parents and fans on that cold Sunday afternoon. The State Finals were about to begin…

Ramapo jumped out to a quick 1-0 lead. In the second half, they increased the lead to 2-0. Soon after, it was 3-0. Ramapo was on their way to the State Championship…

This team, of course, had a collection of outstanding soccer players. It was no surprise Ethan was a bench player. It was special just to be on this team. Yet, Ethan did see his fair share of playing time during the season. He even started one game. This, though, the championship game, was different.

As the game clock went down to under ten minutes left in the contest, I thought about the players, and the decisions the coach would have to make. I know what I would have done; I would have allowed the starters, the star players who brought the team to this point, to remain on the field as they earned the State Title. They deserved it.

And yet…I looked down at the bench and saw one of the coaches talking to my son. I saw Ethan stand up. He took off his sweatshirt, and soon he was standing on the sidelines.

With about six minutes left to play, Coach Baumgarten put in all his seniors, even the back-up players, including the last kid off the bench.

The PA announcer called it, *"Now entering the game for Ramapo, number nine, Ethan Semendinger."* (He even pronounced our name correctly, no small feat!)

Ethan played the remainder of the game and was on the field as his team ended its perfect season.

Marbles

IMPOSSIBLE IS AN ILLUSION

Alex Semendinger is a great kid. All the Semendinger boys are great kids. (Of course, I may be little biased in my assessment.)

Although Alex has many great attributes - he is kind, understanding, funny, smart, hard working, focused - as he grew up, organization was not one of them.

"Alex, is your room clean?" was an often-heard question in the Semendinger house. The follow-up answer, "Yes" also led to an interesting dynamic. Alex's definition of clean, and my definition of clean, were not the same thing.

Growing up, Alex loved marbles. As marbles seemed to be a frequently gifted item, I believe there was a time when he possessed no fewer than 45,765 marbles. Alex's collection contained marbles of various shapes, designs, and colors. Cats-eyes, agates, onionskins, alleys, solids, micas, and peppermint swirls, he had them all. It was an impressive array of marbles.

Part of the problem was that I liked marbles too. They're fun to have and fun to play with. And I like buying things my kids enjoy.

"Hey, look, marbles! I'll get these for Alex!"

Many years ago, Alex's room was more than a bit messy. Part of the clutter involved 42,342 of Alex's marbles. There were marbles everywhere.

Marbles were all over the floor.

There were marbles under the bookshelves.

Marbles were under Alex's desk.

DR. PAUL SEMENDINGER

There were marbles under his bed.

There were even marbles in the bed. If the Guinness World Record people had arrived at our house, we would have been in the running for two accomplishments – The World's Messiest Room and The Most Marbles Ever Scattered Across a Small Area.

From Alex's perspective, his room represented a marble masterpiece.

(Looking back on this, and now forgetting the emotions of the moment, I must say that Alex was probably correct. Never before, or since, were there so many marbles arranged in such a manner. This may have been one of the greatest moments in the history of the world, but now it is lost forever.)

Forty two thousand marbles, and more, were in every possible place.

The marbles had been scattered for days, maybe even weeks.

Of course, I was too lost in the mess to appreciate this singular work of three-dimensional art. Instead I saw a mess and a big one at that.

Marbles were on the window sill.

Marbles were squished between the pages of Alex's books.

There were marbles inside Alex's pillow cases.

There were even marbles inside Alex's pillows. (I still don't know how they got in there.)

And it made me think…

IMPOSSIBLE IS AN ILLUSION

Alex loved his marbles, but I believed that, because he had so many, he didn't appreciate them. The vast quantity of marbles, the myriad marbles, had rendered them, individually, insignificant.

I talked about this with Alex. I asked him if he liked his marbles. He said he did.

I then asked if the way the marbles were scattered demonstrated an appreciation of the marbles. In spite of his possible artist talents and the merits of his creation, he had to agree that they did not.

I then asked, "Alex, if you had only one marble, what would you do with it?"

We talked and thought about that. I suggested that if he had only one marble, he would have treated it with great appreciation – it would have been a cherished possession. I pictured a special box or a special place where that marble would be stored each day after Alex played with it. If Alex had only one marble, I argued, he would treasure that marble as if it were a precious and highly valuable stone.

"Alas!" I said. "It is because of the great abundance of marbles that you fail to value and treasure them." (*I do not believe I really ever said Alas!, but I do like to write it.*)

We live in a materialistic society that is always looking to get more of everything. We love possessing and collecting and gathering and hoarding. We love to say, "I have." And we always seem to want more.

I wonder if we lose something in our desire to have an abundance of everything. I think we do.

What we have in abundance, we do not treasure.

(*I am going to copyright that previous sentence. It may be the most articulate thing I ever wrote. I wrote it, looked back on it, and said aloud, "Wow, that's deep, concise, and to the point. I must have heard it somewhere." So, I typed the words and searched the Internet for them – and no one has said it before. It's my quote. I'm proud of it.*)

What I discovered might rightfully be called The Marble Principle (Or the dear reader might just think, "This author has lost his marbles.").

What we have in abundance, we do not treasure. It's true, not just for marbles, but for most of things we have in life, even the things we don't realize we have.

Take, for example, our health. Do we treasure our health when we're feeling our best?

Or time. When it seems like we have so much of it, do we really value it? It seems to escape us quicker than we realize. I think this applies on so many levels:

The school year, in September and October, seems like it will take a long, long time to complete, and yet, in June, I often wonder, "Where did the time go?"

Childhood is also like this – at least when we view the childhood of others. We always seem to ask, "How did my children get so big, so fast?"

Our own lives – *"I'm HOW old?"* and *"Where did my hair go?"*

Maybe this is where the phrase, "Don't forget to stop and smell the roses" comes from. Maybe the person who said that was saying, "Don't forget to take stock, to cherish the things we have (family,

IMPOSSIBLE IS AN ILLUSION

I recently read a book titled *Finding Zero,* about a mathematician's quest to find the origin of our number system. The tale includes his travels to uncover the civilization that first invented the concept of zero. It is a fascinating book.

I love learning new things. It's a passion. There is just so much knowledge and information out there. When I read, when I study, I am always amazed by the wealth of information that is available to learn – if only we have the time.

I am in awe of what I don't know…

And, I will admit this, before reading the book, I had never heard of the great mathematician Srinivasa Ramanujan. The name meant nothing to me, but that was about to change.

As one reads about numbers and great mathematical thinkers, he is bound to come across Ramanujan. In *Finding Zero,* Ramanujan makes a brief but impressive appearance. The man's sense for numbers and number theory was spellbinding. To be honest, I can't even conceptualize the mathematical principles attributed to Ramanujan, but it is clear that he was a genius. I was immediately taken in by him. Ramanujan leaves an impact.

* * * *

About a month after reading the book, I received an offer for two tickets to a free screening of a brand new movie. No details were provided, but I immediately said "YES" anyway. That night my wife and I were at the AMC Theater in Paramus watching a film titled *"The Man Who Knew Infinity."* It happened to be all about Srinivasa Ramanujan.

I loved the film. As a big fan the Rocky movies, I was disappointed that there were no boxing scenes or scenes of mathematicians sprinting up steps, but otherwise, the movie was great. On the form we had to complete after the screening, I called the movie "Brilliant." That was also what I told the film's producer. "That movie was brilliant," I said.

This was the first time that I had ever been to a Hollywood screening before. It was a great experience. The movie started on time, there were not endless commercials before the film – and there were no previews either. They just showed the movie. It was great.

As I watched the film, I kept thinking, "It was just recently that I never heard of this mathematician and now I'm watching a movie about him – and loving it."

As with most things, there were many lessons in all of this.

First, there is a huge lesson that we must especially share with children – always:

We should never stop learning.

Just when we think we know all about anything, we peek over the horizon and discover that there is a world of information we haven't even begun to tap. There is more knowledge yet to be found. We must never stop trying to learn more. As part of this, we must also always strive to be better. This passion for excellence is what we must share with our students. As educators, it might be the most important thing we can do.

Children must know that they have the ability to learn, that learning is a lifelong process, and that it is the process of learning that makes us great. Learning fuels our potential as individuals and as a society.

IMPOSSIBLE IS AN ILLUSION

It is for this reason that we also never want to cut corners. By striving, by being better than ourselves, by doing more than what is required, we teach children so much more than what is just on the surface. It is why, even in challenging times, we need to continue to set the highest bar.

When we stop doing our best and when we begin to rely on our past successes, we begin to erode our future reputations. People don't want to hear how great a program was two years ago. Or what we did five years ago. Or yesterday. They want to know what we did for their kids *today*. It is through our continued quest for excellence that we forge our great reputations.

But, back to Ramanujan…

Ramanujan's biggest challenge, at least according to the movie, was not that he wasn't a gifted mathematician. His challenge was that his line of thinking and reasoning, possibly because of his background in India, was not congruent with the great minds of western culture at Trinity College in Cambridge.

While it seems that much of his mathematical reasoning was solid – and that the theorems he developed were correct, he did not have the "proofs" that western thought asked of him and needed from him.

Ramanujan struggled with trying to think as a westerner and provide proofs for mathematical concepts that he seemed to figure out in a different way.

It wasn't that he was wrong. It was that this thinking was different.

As a pre-schooler, my youngest son Ethan could do all sorts of mathematical computations in his head. Ethan understood (in his own way) carrying numbers, double digit addition and subtraction, and even some basic multiplication and division. He knew these things in his head.

Then, of course, he went to school. Somehow, somewhere, Ethan's ability to think as he did mathematically was lost. As he learned the standard formulas in school, Ethan's talent to solve equations in his head, his own way, disappeared.

Now, maybe my son's original math had limitations. Maybe his math wouldn't have allowed him to advance beyond what he already knew. Maybe the math he was taught opened his mind in new and better ways. We'll never know. All I do know is that "our math" (the math of school) turned off my son's own way of correctly solving equations.

Ramanujan faced this problem at a higher level with the most detailed of mathematical reasoning. Ramanujan was solving some of the most challenging mathematical questions of the day, but he didn't have the proofs to demonstrate how or why he knew what he did. Ramanujan understood math in a different way than the "experts," and because his thinking was different, they discounted him and told him he was wrong.

I'll admit, I'm not enough of a mathematician to understand or explain Ramanujan's thinking beyond this most simplistic outline, but it does bring me, finally, to the main point.

I think that sometimes, in our quests to teach a certain way, or follow a specific program, we actually stifle learning. We often say things to children such as, "You have to show your work" because that's what has always been done. For some kids, trying to think "our" way might actually be a hindrance.

IMPOSSIBLE IS AN ILLUSION

The movie made me think that, at least with some students, maybe we need to accept the idea that they just do know the answers. Maybe there are times they don't need to "show the work."

Ramanujan stumbled when powerful thinkers in his world of mathematics made him "show the work" in the way they wanted the work to be shown. The experts thought their ways were always correct. They might not have been.

Today, there may be times when students say, "I know the answer," and they actually do, but they can't necessary explain how or why they know it. And that it might be ok.

I can ride a bike. I cannot explain, in the least bit, how or why. I don't understand the principles or the physics that make riding a bike possible. I just know how to do it. It might be that way with some kids and math or science, or anything. There are times when they might just know.

Maybe, sometimes, by continually asking for reasoning and proof we're pulling against a soaring thought and a creative mind. Instead, we must continue to find ways that allow children to think and reason in profound ways. When we do this, we might be giving children the tools that allows them to soar.

In doing so, by getting out of their way, we might be doing our very best teaching.

A Little Lesson in Latin

IMPOSSIBLE IS AN ILLUSION

*T*here is a Latin phrase that reads, *"Crede quod habes, et habes."*

This can be translated as, "Believe that you have it, and you have it."

As we look to find ways to (continually) improve student performance, the key might be in that little Latin phrase.

"Believe that you can do it."

I have always found that by telling people they can do things, they have found that they can… do things. It's a pretty simple formula. When you think you can, you can. Confidence and belief are strong motivators.

I know when people have believed in me, I have often tried very hard to make their belief a reality. Most often I have rewarded their confidence in me by achieving what they thought was possible, which was not necessarily what I originally thought was possible.

As I think of many of my life's "accomplishments," each time there was a person, or people, that said, "Paul, you can do it." These encouragers made me believe in myself.

Today, when I have self doubts about being able to accomplish a task, I think about the faith others have in me. This often leads me to say, "I can do it." And I usually do!

In a few weeks I'll be struggling on the streets of New York City as I run the New York City Marathon. There is something glorious, magical, wonderful (and horrible, painful, upsetting, and ugly) about struggling through the New York City Marathon. I am (just about) ready for the race. Throughout the long training process I often have to tell myself, "You can do it." Along with this, I have family members and friends who encourage me throughout my training.

And don't be fooled, no matter how prepared I might be, there are always periods of doubt.

I have participated in many races and have been a spectator at many others. You might be surprised, but encouraging words, even from a stranger, such as, "YOU CAN DO IT!" or "YOU LOOK GREAT" or "I BELIEVE IN YOU" can have an amazing impact on a runner's state of mind – even when that runner is in the depth of misery. Words like that have helped me find something deep inside and push through the disbelief I have in myself.

BELIEVE THAT YOU HAVE IT, AND YOU HAVE IT.

Could it be possible that these nine English words (or six Latin words) hold the ultimate key to success?

If strangers can impact on a runner's performance (and I know that this helps many, not just me) – imagine the impact of a child's teacher? We have said, often, that the teacher is one of the biggest influencers in a child's life. Our words are powerful. Our actions speak volumes.

Imagine then, the power of these words spoken to individuals and groups:

BELIEVE YOU CAN DO IT, AND YOU CAN DO IT.

In 1973, the New York Mets had a remarkable pennant run that was inspired, in part, from the words of pitcher Tug McGraw. He said simply, "Ya Gotta Believe."

The Mets did believe – and they took that belief all the way to the World Series against the longest of odds.

IMPOSSIBLE IS AN ILLUSION

As we create ignition for children, as we inspire them to learn, as we motivate them, we must remember to continually tell them:

"YOU CAN DO IT!"

Then, take it even one step further. Tell them not just that they can do it, but, tell them:

"I BELIEVE YOU CAN DO IT," and "I BELIEVE IN YOU."

Those just might be the most powerful words any person can tell another person.

"I believe in you."

When we tell our students that we believe in them, they will believe us and believe in themselves. They will give that extra effort. They will rise above their own fears or skepticism.

The results will be spectacular!

Another Lesson in Latin
◆

IMPOSSIBLE IS AN ILLUSION

Let's now look at another Latin phrase - *"Carpe diem."*

This phrase is popular in literature and was a major theme in the movie *Dead Poets Society*. *Carpe diem* might be the most famous Latin phrase today.

According to conventional wisdom, the words mean "Seize the Day!" But, in actuality, they mean more than that. The phrase's origins, it seems, comes from the Roman poet Horace who wrote: *"Dum loquimur, fugerit invida Aetas: carpe diem, quam minimum credula postero."* Scholars translate this as, "While we're talking, envious time is fleeing: pluck the day, put no trust in the future." In other words, "Live for today, you don't know what tomorrow will bring."

Now, I would posit that living too much for today can bring dangerous consequences. Further, I would argue that Horace wasn't necessarily advocating for that. He asked us to make the most of the present, to "seize the day," but only as part of preparing for our endless tomorrows.

Carpe diem is a credo I live by. I certainly attempt to seize each day. I work diligently and passionately to find ways to be my best self. I am continually striving and continually reaching... (And those who know me best also know that I fail in all of this much more often than I succeed.)

In my professional life, I believe that one reason my school is so highly regarded is because the entire staff has also always embraced this philosophy. The school's reputation is one of caring and compassionate teachers who work diligently and passionately for children. Because these educators look beyond themselves in their planning and lesson delivery and they make the time to relate with the children, they most certainly "Seize the Day." It was through this passion for excellence that the love, respect, and admiration for the school was born and grew, and it is because the teachers continue to give of themselves, that the school's reputation continues to flourish.

But we must be cautious. We must pause. We must reflect…because there is a bigger issue that goes along with this.

One of the hard facts, not just of education, but of life, is that we have to confirm our reputations daily. We cannot seize just one day; we must seize each and every day.

We cannot, in any profession, sit back and rest on our laurels. It is always the right time to give our best efforts, to make the most of ourselves, and to set the highest standards. Our reputation does not get enhanced by what we did yesterday, instead it grows by what we are doing now.

This fact can be seen in sports all of the time. Today's hero is tomorrow's doormat.

A perfect example of this occurred with the New York Yankees during their furious drive to the American League East Pennant in 2012. As the season drew to a close, the Yankees' second baseman Robinson Cano was on an unbelievable hot streak. He was seemingly hitting everything that was pitched to him. Each at-bat promised, and produced, some type of heroic. Cano helped the Yankees finish the season in first place. Article after article was written about how Robinson Cano was the "Next Great Yankees Legend." People were saying he should earn the Most Valuable Player Award.

But then the playoffs began and Robinson Cano's bat disappeared. At one point he set a record for consecutive at-bats without a hit. Cano wasn't just bad – he was legendarily bad. At that point, article after article was published about how the Yankees needed to start again and how they need to rid themselves of this awful player.

IMPOSSIBLE IS AN ILLUSION

Within just a few weeks, the feelings about Robinson Cano changed drastically.

Like fickle baseball fans, parents do not necessarily care about that great project a class did last year, they want to know what the class is doing this year for their kid. That is one of the great challenges of our profession – but it is also one of the things that makes our profession so great. We have to keep on our toes, we have to continually be our best – because it isn't just about us, it is about the children we are expected to educate each and every day.

Baseball often mirrors life. If we look for bad things, we will find them. We can find things to bemoan in any workplace and in any situation. I have read stories about athletes, Wall Street workers, and even employees at Disney World that find faults in their work environment.

But if we look to what is good, we can also find the good. Lost in all the upset over the Yankees' poor playoff performance in 2012 was the fact that over the course of the long baseball season (162 games over 6 months), the Yankees were the very best team in the league. No team in the American League won more games than the Yankees in 2012. There was a lot about the Yankees to be excited about. People just decided to stop looking for the good.

Seize the day? Of course.

We become our best selves when we give our best to others. When we see that the world is bigger than our own needs we can find the energy to give even more of ourselves.

When we seize the day, we are creating a certain magic that helps make the world a better place - one moment at a time.

Seize the day, not to just live recklessly, but to uplift others.

DR. PAUL SEMENDINGER

You see, when you bring out the best in others, you are really bringing out the best parts of yourself.

A Third Lesson in Latin

IMPOSSIBLE IS AN ILLUSION

*T*here is a Latin phrase that reads, *"Vivere cotidie cras in mente."*

The previous phrase, *"Carpe diem"* was originally coined by the legendary Roman poet Horace. This next phrase was first coined, I believe, by a philosopher and writer of much more minor significance. This writer grew up in the 20th century and goes by the name of Semendinger.

(I am not sure I actually coined this phrase, but I think I did, and even if I didn't, it's my piece so I am going to claim that I did. Author's Privilege or Creative License… call it what you wish.)

In its original English (it was only recently translated into Latin – about two minutes ago) the phrase reads, *"Live each day with tomorrow in mind."*

Live each day with tomorrow in mind.

When I was a middle school principal, I started using this phrase as an intentional contrast to the prevalent middle and high school philosophy of "Live for Today." I found that the "Live for Today" school of thought often led to destructive behavior. The "live each moment as if it were your last" approach has led to many disastrous tomorrows.

And I also know all too well about the children who "lived for today" and didn't get to see a tomorrow.

It was because of these concerns that I began telling the graduating eighth grade students of my school, "Live each day with tomorrow in mind." Our entire life, except for that one fateful day when it all ends, is full of tomorrows. You cannot go back and change yesterday, but you sure can plan and make the best decisions to allow for the hope that tomorrow will always be better.

Living each day with tomorrow in mind is the thought I referenced, briefly, in the previous passage when we were "seizing the day." I truly believe that we must seize each day. *Carpe diem!* But we should not seize the individual day, or the individual moment, at the expense of the future – or of a better tomorrow.

We should always try to make tomorrow better because of what we did today. As such, we can seize the day, and we can grab the moment, but as we do so, we have to remember that tomorrow also counts. To attain better tomorrows, we have to make our todays the very best they can be. As we do this, we don't have to start big. Great change sometimes comes in very small steps.

I think this is, at its heart, is what teaching really is. The children in our midst have more tomorrows than we do. It is our job to help them have the very best tomorrows. In order to set children up for their hopeful futures, we instruct and we teach. In order to make the students' tomorrows as bright as they can be, we set good examples for hard work, for focus, for pushing our boundaries... by striving to be our best. We teach kids that they can always be better. We encourage kids to continually improve. We support children as they struggle along the way.

We do all of this to try to promise each student a bright future.

As educators, we constantly look ahead – and teach children to do the same – because tomorrow holds great promise. Living totally for the moment doesn't give that promise. In fact, living in the moment is really a false promise – it means that a person lives for a time that is already expiring.

We shouldn't live for now, or what came before; instead, we should live for what is to come. A full life is one that is continually anticipating, ever looking hopefully ahead. Make the most of today,

IMPOSSIBLE IS AN ILLUSION

but prepare and look forward to what comes next. For as good as today is, tomorrow can be ever greater.

The Beatles sang with sadness about "Yesterday." This is typical. Songs written about the past are usually filled with melancholy.

In the play *Annie*, the hope is for "Tomorrow" because that's when the proverbial sun will come out. Tomorrow is always brighter.

The very basic reason for schools are to help each child, and ultimately society, have better tomorrows.

As such, we need to work hard today to build the skills we will need tomorrow.

We give our best today because tomorrow is counting on us! In order for tomorrow to truly be Tomorrow, it needs our very best today.

The efforts we give, the extras we do, the gifts we provide, the love we share, the positive choices we make, and the passion we bring… that's part of seizing the day. But more, it's living each day with tomorrow in mind.

Vivere cotidie cras in mente!

I Love To Read

IMPOSSIBLE IS AN ILLUSION

I love to read. Reading opens minds to new ideas. Reading transports us to faraway places – real or imagined. Reading allows us to go back in time and learn from the past. Through reading we can imagine the future. Reading can ground us. It can teach us how to think and feel. Reading can also spark our imaginations and allow us to figure out things we never thought possible – or possibly never even imagined.

To read is to open a mind forever.

Through books, I have walked on the moon, played for the Yankees, battled evil wizards, fought in the Civil War, grown spiritually, learned about love, discovered new ideas, laughed, cried, lost sleep, made people offers they can't refuse, knocked out the heavyweight champion, stayed gold, hated phonies, met Boo Radley, hiked the Appalachian Trail, run a four-minute mile, let them build it, on and on, and so much more.

I have learned about words and space; mathematics and baseball (and how intertwined these two really are); love and compassion; good guys and bad guys; politicians (I think I just mentioned them); heroes and villains (maybe this is also redundant)…

I have read a plethora of great books that have inspired and taught me about quality education, effective leadership, and forward thinking. I have learned how to become creative, understand the brain, become more mindful…on and on, and so much more,

I think it is safe to say that it is through our thirst for knowledge that we grow as human beings. Through reading we become our better selves.

When one stops reading, I believe, one stops growing. A closed mind is like a closed door. When we read, we realize that there is always something more to learn. We also find that there are different perspectives on things that we may have never questioned.

We learn that we're not always right.

Books open doors to thoughts, ideas, revelations, epiphanies…on and on, and so much more.

I love when I find a great book that I just can't put down. I devour books like that. I recently read a fantastic book, *The Life And Times of the Thunderbolt Kid,* by Bill Bryson (one of my favorite writers). I think I read it cover to cover, all four hundred pages, in about 35 minutes. (At least it felt that way.) I love a book that I enjoy so much that I cannot put it down.

Conversely, I sometimes get frustrated when I am bogged down in a book that I just can't seem to finish. Right now I am still fighting the Civil War with Ulysses S. Grant as I plod my way through his *Memoirs*. It's not that the book isn't well written. It's actually great. Sometimes, though, it feels as if I am actually with Grant as he slowly moves his armies forward and prepares for a siege. Petersburg is just ahead. I am already digging my trench in anticipation. (Once I finish that book, 600+ pages of small print, I will feel very accomplished. It has been a challenging, but very engaging read.)

I must also admit that there are times when I just can't finish a book for one reason or another. At home I have a list of books I wanted to love and just couldn't. I have found that some books are worth giving up on - although I never feel good when that happens. There are too many great books in the world for me to waste time on the ones I don't enjoy. The good news is that I always find a better alternative.

* * * *

IMPOSSIBLE IS AN ILLUSION

I can get lost in book stores. Sometimes I wish they would lock me up in a book store for a month (in the winter please, I don't want to miss a ballgame or a great day to run outside) so that I can do nothing but read and read and read.

(I also love to write. I often feel envious of all the authors that have been published as I walk around book stores. I imagine that one of life's great feelings will be to walk past a book shelf in Barnes and Noble and see a bunch of books that I wrote.) (It will happen!)

I love used book sales even more than book stores. One can build a huge library in moments at a used book sale. I love picking up a book that others have passed by quickly and discovering that it is one that I enjoy immensely. Some of the best books I have ever read have been found at used book sales. I have a large collection of books at home. Most I purchased second-hand.

And libraries! What is better than a library? You go there, browse all their items, pick a few out, and they let you take them home, for free, as long as you promise to bring the items back. How cool is that? I find libraries to be some of the most amazing places anywhere.

Books, they're great.

* * * *

I have noticed, however, that my love of books has a limitation. When I find a book I want to read, at a library, or a book store, or a sale, I can't wait to open the cover and start enjoying each word. But when someone else tells me to read something, as good as the book might be, it sometimes seems like a chore. In these situations, it sometimes seems that I'm reading the book for someone else rather than for myself.

This is especially true if the book was assigned to me to read – whether in a class or at work. "You are required to read this" are words I greatly dislike hearing. They signify to me that someone is stealing my time.

I remember back in high school being resistant to almost any book my teachers assigned. "If it's for school," I thought, "it can't be good." (*The Catcher in the Rye* was a notable exception. I couldn't wait to read that book and I loved every word.) Those feelings changed a bit as I matured, but, sometimes they still pop up.

But if we only read the things we find or the things we want to read ourselves, we lose out on so much. Sometimes we need to be encouraged, or forced, to step outside our comfort zones and encounter books that we would have never chosen on our own. I know I do.

I used to ask my friends to recommend their favorite books to me. I read some great books that way. One friend, though, recommended *Of Human Bondage* by W. Somerset Maugham. Ironically, I had always wanted to read that book, so I set out to do so. I think the copy I had was over 800 pages long, but it might have been a thousand, or maybe a million. While I enjoyed the book, it took me a lifetime to read it. As I slogged through, I couldn't stop thinking about all the other great books I was missing out on. When I completed the text, I approached my friend and told him that I enjoyed the story well enough, but also commented that it was an extremely long book. My friend replied, "Oh, I read the abridged version."

Most often today, when I'm given a book, my first reaction is to be thankful. This isn't always the case, but I try to make it the case more and more often.

IMPOSSIBLE IS AN ILLUSION

In spite of my usual initial resistance, over the years I have learned a lot about a lot by reading books that were assigned or recommended to me. One example is the book *A Whole New Mind* by Daniel Pink. I opened the book reluctantly, but, as always, with a glimmer of hope, and ended up devouring each word. The book was better than I could have ever imagined. It influenced me in countless ways. I am still a big fan of Dan Pink and I read everything he now writes.

As I mentioned above, one of my favorite writers is Bill Bryson, but I didn't discover him for myself; rather, my oldest son Ryan recommended a Bryson book to me…and I became an instant fan. My library (purchased mostly from used book sales) now contains almost everything Bryson has ever written. I look forward to reading each of those books!

I can't get enough of books.

Know any good ones?

(Apollo) Credo

◆

IMPOSSIBLE IS AN ILLUSION

*E*ach year, on January 1, our local newspaper, the *Bergen Record*, begins the year by outlining their editorial philosophy so it is plain and clear for all their readers.

Although I believe I make my philosophies pretty clear and that my positions on most things are well-known and apparent to my staff, I figured it would be good for me to participate in a similar exercise. It is good to be both self-reflective and also to take the time to outline one's beliefs.

As such, what follows is my credo – my philosophies on life, work, and being one's best.

POSITIVITY – This is my constant theme. I do not believe anything can be accomplished without enthusiasm and a sincere desire to find the good in (almost) everything. I have never heard of any person who achieved success through a poor attitude or through negativity. Work is work, life is life, and there are always aspects of each that people can find things to disagree with. Nothing is perfect. No one is perfect. But there is no point in dwelling on the negative. Instead, I like to find examples of how positive approaches have helped others and rectified situations. Hearing about others' successes motivates me to work even harder. I believe that success begets success. I also believe that a positive outlook is the key to a successful organization, a productive work environment, and a happy life. I like to look for the good – everywhere. When I find it, it serves as a reminder that there can be good in everything.

PERSPECTIVE – I am motivated by stories of success. When I hear examples of how others have overcome great or grave challenges, I am inspired. I am also humbled. I am often reminded that many of my own concerns are small in comparison to what other people have gone through. (Think your job is tough? Imagine spending three weeks in a fox hole, surrounded by the enemy during the coldest winter in European history without proper food, clothing, or ammunition. Imagine watching your friends dying from cold or enemy gun fire. Imagine the cold dark nights. Imagine Christmas Morning, 1944. This is what it was like for American soldiers at Bastogne during what would be called The Battle of the Bulge. None of my problems compare in any way to that.) For me, learning about how others have overcome grave difficulties helps make the trials and tribulations I face at work or life feel minor in comparison. During my daily work life, as stressful or challenging as a situation might be, I know that many people have it much harder, each and every day.

In addition to being inspired by how others have overcome huge challenges, I am also reminded how fortunate I am to have what I have. I am fortunate to have a great job, a happy family, great friends and colleagues, and to live a life free from want. My goodness, I am very fortunate!

PROFESSIONAL GROWTH – I believe that growth is a major component of professionalism. I use many avenues for self-growth. I read, I study, and I attend lectures and conferences. I talk as often as I can to successful people and professionals whom I admire. I am often humbled (I get humbled a lot) when I do this because it makes me realize all the ways I still fall short.

But maybe my best character trait is that I understand my many weaknesses and I have a true desire to grow.

An interesting aspect of reading is that rather than quenching my desire to acquire information, the more I read, no matter the subject, the more I thirst for more. Knowledge and understanding are things I crave. Reading reminds me that I have so much yet to learn.

IMPOSSIBLE IS AN ILLUSION

I also write as a way to challenge myself to critically think about my philosophies and my actions. I have learned a lot about myself by reflecting on a great deal through writing. When I write about situations and decisions I have made, it gives me the time and the focus to look critically at my own decision making. Writing is an excellent tool for self-growth.

At times, I challenge the teachers I work with to look at alternative approaches to instruction. I like to share the words of experts and others who inspire me. There have been times when teachers have felt uneasy by this. Change is not a bad thing – it helps us grow. If we're never challenged, how can we improve? And if we're not willing to improve, how can we ask that of our students?

I have found, in every area of my life, that the people who are the most successful are the ones most critical of themselves. There is always room to grow. We must always strive to be better.

LOVE – Most of all, I believe in love. It's the over-reaching theme of everything I write about. I love to read. I love to write. I love baseball and the Rocky movies. I love to run. I love to help others. I love my family and friends. I love God.

When we love, we humble ourselves. When we love, we give of ourselves. When we love, we realize that we can always do better.

But, also when we love, we bring joy. We bring happiness. We bring kindness and appreciation and understanding.

It is because I love my job that I work so hard at it. It is because I love the teachers that I put pressure on myself to be better. I strive to make the school environment the best place for them. It is because I love students, and see the goodness in every child, and am in awe of their potential, that I try to never see the time I spend at work as work. It's not. Educators are given a gift – the gift to be present as young lives develop. We're able to shape the future. We are given the gift of helping children find goodness and value in themselves and in others.

When we look for the good, we can always find it.

When we truly love, we often find that we are motivated to grow and to care and to be positive.

And when we love, others love us back.

The Eagle and the Owl

IMPOSSIBLE IS AN ILLUSION

If you came into my office, the first thing you might notice is a large collection of objects displayed on the shelves – and actually all over. There's the standard principal's office fare: books and binders and photos. And lots of papers. But in addition, there's also a plethora of other things: toys, stuffed animals, plaques, trophies, and signs. All of my favorite interests seem to be represented. The Yankees, the Marx Brothers, the Beatles, Disney, Superheroes, Rocky, and the Charlie Brown gang are all on display in one way or another.

I guess all of this makes my office seem a little more like home. (It should after all; there are long periods of time where I spend more hours at work than in my house.)

As for the toys, well, I am a kid at heart. I also think that toys help the students feel a little more comfortable in my office. After all, kids love toys. It helps when the principal does as well. (At least I think it helps…)

Two items that sometimes seem out of place among this collection are two birds carved out of wood – an eagle and an owl. When visitors ask about the items I have on display, they most often ask about the eagle and owl.

Interestingly, if I were decorating a room from scratch, I would probably not choose these items for myself. I'm actually not a big fan of birds. In fact, I greatly dislike a whole number of Orioles and Blue Jays (forgive, please, the baseball pun). One bird that I do like is the cardinal. Cardinals are very pretty – and the cardinal was the mascot of Pompton Lakes High School, a wonderful school where I served as vice principal many years ago. I loved that school and in that light, having a cardinal on display might make some sense. But I don't have any cardinals.

These other birds, the wooden eagle and the wooden owl, also come from my time at Pompton Lakes High School. They were given to me by a most special person at the school, a man who I think about almost daily, and who was one of the most influential people in my life: Mr. Ernie Fisher, the principal who hired me. During my years as the vice principal of Pompton Lakes High School, Mr. Fisher served as my mentor, my friend, and as a person I looked up to in every way.

I don't look like the typical high school vice principal type. I'm short. I'm not at all intimidating. And I smile a lot – some would say too much. I looked even less like a vice principal when I assumed the position as a twenty-eight-year-old coming right out of a middle school social studies classroom. To some of the veteran staff, I looked more like a student than an administrator. (I even had a full head of hair back then.)

It was a huge transition for me to go from teaching to administration. I think I did well enough right from the start, but it wasn't always easy. (Is it ever?) I loved being a teacher. (I used to say that no one loved teaching as much as I did, but over the years I have found many people who share that love – especially in the school that I proudly serve as principal today). I always want to push myself to try new and greater things, and I do, but making the career change from teacher to administrator was quite a large transition for me.

Throughout that time, Mr. Fisher was always there to offer support, give guidance, and even lend a helping hand.

There were many days, too many to count, where he and I would talk about the issues of the school, the concerns of the day, or just education in general well into the evenings. Mr. Fisher never grew short with me. His door was always open. He freely gave of his time. And, as I have learned, this trait is something not found in most other leaders. Mr. Fisher cared about the school, the students, the teachers, and every member of the support staff. His words and actions inspired me, made me see how much I had to learn, and taught me the true definition of empathy.

I've never known such a smart, well read, introspective, and philosophical person as Mr. Fisher. He was able to challenge and inspire me in a supportive and nonjudgmental manner. I often sought his advice in the challenging world of high school discipline. He gave his thoughts freely, but always said, "Paul, you know best. As the vice principal, you are the only one who truly knows all the facts."

How inspiring it was to be trusted, absolutely, by this master educator and sage!

It may sound like a contrast, but Mr. Fisher was also a man of few words. As I reflect on many of our conversations, I remember being the person doing much of the talking, and sometimes through this, working through the problems by myself. And yet, it was always Mr. Fisher's knowing smile, encouragement, and support that allowed me the ability to think through the biggest challenges I faced.

Mr. Fisher also didn't give praise lightly. A "Good Job" from Mr. Fisher was priceless. The emotion I try to evoke from others by saying something like, "That was the most awesome, spectacularly amazing thing I've ever seen in the history of forever!" doesn't carry the same weight, even today, that a simple "Good Job" from Mr. Fisher did.

(At this point the dear reader says, "I wish Mr. Fisher taught Paul brevity.")

Mr. Fisher ranks as one of the finest people I have ever known. I treasured our working relationship. I consider myself very fortunate indeed to have been able to share a few years of my life with him. I am a better principal because I knew Mr. Fisher.

More, I'm a better human being.

There are not enough Ernie Fishers in the world.

When I left Pompton Lakes High School to become the principal of a middle school in another district, Mr. Fisher gave the owl and the eagle to me as gifts. He explained that he usually didn't give gifts to people but wanted to do so on this occasion. I was touched. I still am. I often wonder if I meant as much to him as he did to me, but it can't be so.

When he handed me the birds, still wrapped in a box, Mr. Fisher said that he wanted to give me a gift that had meaning.

In the card that he gave along with the birds, Mr. Fisher simply wrote,

> *"May courage and wisdom always lead you to do the right."*

...and those are the words I try to live by each and every day. I still have the card in which he inscribed those words. It sits in my top drawer. I look at it often.

It's been over twenty years since I left Pompton Lakes High School. In that time I have grown from a kid to a man. I've raised my own family. I've been the educational leader of wonderful two schools. I give motivational talks. I write about being one's best – and about love and compassion and understanding. People now come to me for advice. (Some people actually think I know what I am talking about.)

IMPOSSIBLE IS AN ILLUSION

Each day I have to make challenging decisions. There are issues that face children, teachers, secretaries, custodians, and parents. None of this is easy. Every situation directly impacts someone's life. It's a huge responsibility. I don't think many truly understand how much passes by a principal's desk in a given day.

Often times I don't want to make the hard choices that fall on me. It can be lonely at the top. No matter how many years I do my job, some decisions never get easier. Sometimes I'd rather pick up a toy and be a kid again. Sometimes I'd rather just go for a run.

Sometimes I just want to cry.

But then I look to the eagle and the owl.

The eagle reminds me to have courage; the owl reminds me to be wise. Together, they inspire me to "do the right." Often times, the right thing is the most challenging. The right thing always requires more work. And frequently, the right thing involves the most heartache.

But the right thing is still what we must do - always.

Mr. Fisher taught me a great deal. He taught me what it means to lead. The Eagle and Owl, they serve to remind me of this each and every day.

DR. PAUL SEMENDINGER

The Story of a Winner
(Meb Keflezighi)

DR. PAUL SEMENDINGER

*I*t is probably somewhat normal, even for adults, to have favorite sports figures that they root for. Baseball, football, and hockey players, tennis and golf stars, auto racers and others come to mind. However, there are probably few people who closely follow the career of a professional runner.

I am one of those people. I am fan of Meb Keflezighi. He's a champion marathoner.

But it hasn't always been that way.

*****

A few years ago, I had the pleasure of meeting Meb Keflezighi at a New York Road Runners event. It was a special thrill because it is not often that I get to meet famous people. I found Meb delightful. He was patient and made time for each person who wished to talk with him. I was amazed that he had a conversation with me. In that conversation, I invited him to come speak to the children at my school.

I'm still hoping he takes me up on that offer.

*****

The story of Meb Keflezighi inspires me to always strive for greatness and to always give my best. Meb's career illustrates that failure is not permanent. In addition, Meb has proven that you can be a winner even if you sometimes fall short of your goals.

For many years, despite intensive training and a lot of promise, Meb continually failed in his ultimate goal – winning a marathon. For a long period, he was the perennial also-ran - the runner-up. Meb was the elite marathoner who couldn't win a big race.

Some people feel that "Second place is the first loser." And second place was where Meb found himself – seemingly quite often. And then…it got worse. He wasn't even finishing in second.

But, as I often do, I am getting ahead of myself. So, let's start at the beginning.

This is a story of Meb Keflezighi.

* * * *

Mebrahtom Keflezighi immigrated to the United States from Eritrea when he was twelve years old. He ran some competitions in junior high school (winning a few) and then as a high school student in 1994, he won the California State High School Championships in the 1600 meters *and* the 3200 meters.

Meb then attended UCLA where he became a four time national champion. It was during his time at UCLA that he set the American record for the 10,000 meters. His career was on fast forward!

It was at this point that Meb set his sights on the next big challenge – the marathon.

People predicted greatness. Meb was hailed as *"The American Who Would Finally Win a Major Marathon."* (For most of its history, marathon running has been dominated by runners from countries other than the United States. It was hoped that Meb would buck this trend.)

So it began.

In 2002, Meb ran his first marathon, the New York City Marathon and finished in ninth place. For a first race, especially in New York, that was a very respectable showing.

In 2003, Meb ran the Chicago Marathon… and came in seventh. He was getting better.

In 2004, Meb entered the USA Olympic Trials for the Marathon Team. This time he came in second and earned a spot on the United States Olympic team.

Later, in the 2004 Summer Olympics in Athens, Greece, Meb finished second again, winning the Silver Medal. It was a glorious run and a fantastic display of Meb's skills as a runner. Meb's finish was the first time since 1976 that an American had medaled in an Olympic Marathon.

Just 70 days later, Meb ran the NYC Marathon and came in… second place.

In other words, in 2004, Meb ran three marathons and had three second place finishes. He was on the precipice of greatness. It seemed like he was now ready to win a big race.

2005 arrived. Meb again competed in the New York City Marathon. This time he dropped a spot and came in third.

In 2006, Meb ran the Boston Marathon and, again, came in third.

Meb's next big race was the 2006 New York City Marathon. Many predicted that this would finally be his break-out race. It wasn't.

IMPOSSIBLE IS AN ILLUSION

In that race, Meb finished in 21st place. A disaster. Failure.

The following year, 2007, brought more struggles and even more challenges. Meb entered the London Marathon and was unable to finish. Every marathoner's nightmare is the dreaded DNF (Did Not Finish). Meb now had one of those on his record.

Undeterred, Meb entered the USA Olympic Trials again. He finished in an unremarkable eighth place and failed to make the team. Worse, during this competition he suffered a pelvic stress fracture that left him unable to walk. And even worse still, his friend and fellow marathoner Ryan Shay died while competing in that race.

Meb did not compete in a marathon in 2008. Instead, after failing in his hopes to run the marathon, he entered the Olympic Trials for the 10,000 meters, a race he used to dominate when he was a three-time USA champion. Meb came in 13$^{th.}$ He failed to qualify. There would be no Olympics at any race distance for Meb Keflezighi in 2008. In four short years, Meb Keflezighi went being an Olympic Silver Medalist to not even being able to make the Olympic team.

Most often, elite marathoners don't have long careers of sustained greatness. The distance is grueling. The training and the racing taxes the body. Most elites only run one to two major races a year. To stay at the top of their field is extremely difficult. There always seems to be a faster, younger, better trained runner, ready to capture the top prize.

It had been a long time since Meb had even been close to the top prize.

By the end of 2008, it seemed that Meb Keflezighi might never be a marathon champion or any type of champion again. His greatest days seemed well behind him.

2009 arrived. That year began with Meb racing in the London Marathon. His previous attempt in London resulted in a race he could not complete. This time he finished. But, he still only came in 9th place.

In November 2009, Meb ran the New York City Marathon again. Before the race, he was not considered to have much of a chance. Other marathoners, like Ryan Hall (The *Next* Great American Hope), were the favorites. The television coverage did even not pay much attention to Meb. No one seriously considered him to be a challenger.

But, when the race started, he went out with the leaders and he stayed with them. At five kilometers, he was within a second or two of the leading runners and through sheer will or skill, he remained at the front, mile after mile. Meb and the lead group were within four seconds of the leader at the half-way mark (13.1 miles).

The second half of a marathon is where champions are made. Meb stayed with the leaders. Then the lead pack started getting smaller. Soon it became a two-man race. Determined, Meb pushed forward, and with only a few miles to go, when Meb entered Central Park, the place where his friend Ryan Shay died, he rushed ahead to the front.

Well, this story has a predictable ending. You should anticipate it by now. Meb won! Meb was the New York City Marathon Champion! After years of disappointment and failure, Meb finally won the big race!

In winning, Meb Keflezighi became the first American since 1972 to win this epic endurance event.

****

IMPOSSIBLE IS AN ILLUSION

People talk a lot about how athletes should "go out on top." One could argue that the New York City Marathon is distance running's Super Bowl, so a victory there might have been a great time for Meb to retire. But he didn't.

And success also didn't always follow Meb either.

Meb was on hand to defend his NYC victory in the 2010 marathon. He finished in sixth place.

In 2011, he finished in sixth again in New York.

It seemed like the same old pattern was emerging.

But then came the 2012 United States Olympic Trials in Houston, Texas. To everyone's surprise, this race saw Meb once again taking the top honors. Like a phoenix emerging from the ashes, Meb Keflezighi rose again!

That summer, in the London Olympics, Meb did not earn a medal, but he came in fourth place and was the highest finisher for the United States.

Due to Hurricane Sandy, there was no NYC Marathon in 2012. But in 2013, Meb once again ran the New York City Marathon...and came in 23rd place. He was never a major factor in the race.

Had Meb's time finally come – and gone? At 38 years old, it seemed that, this time, once and for all, Meb's winning days were over.

And then he did it again!

In 2014, in an extremely emotional and inspirational race, Meb Keflezighi won the Boston Marathon. He was the first American to win that race in 31 years!

In 2015, Meb finished eighth in Boston and seventh in New York, but he wasn't quite done yet.

With one more Olympics on the horizon, Meb Keflezighi laced up his running shoes to compete one last time to represent the United States in an Olympic marathon. He was forty years old and had to battle in the largest field of racers ever assembled for an American Olympic Marathon Trial.

And when that race ended as well, Meb Keflezighi was on the podium. He earned an impressive third place finish to qualify for the team.

In the 2016 Olympics, Meb finished in a distant thirty-third place, but he battled among and with the best in world.

In 2017, Meb will run the Boston Marathon and the New York City Marathon and then retire. Oh what a career it was!

* * * *

This story of Meb Keflezighi is one of perseverance. Perseverance is defined by the Meriam-Webster Dictionary as, "continued effort to do something despite difficulties, failure, or opposition."

Perseverance is a common theme that I write about – always trying, always striving, never giving up. As long as there is a drive and a desire to improve - no matter what the odds – success is right around the corner. Success is always attainable.

In spite of many difficulties, great obstacles, and a series of failures, Meb Keflezighi always pushed forward. It's this drive that inspires me. It's this attitude that I hope to continue to teach others.

IMPOSSIBLE IS AN ILLUSION

Meb Keflezighi's story shows that persistence and perseverance pays off.

And, as long as each of us always gives our best, like Meb, we will also always be champions!

DR. PAUL SEMENDINGER

Baron von Steuben

Over the years, I have planned, organized, and led our local Boy Scout troop on many trips to historical places. I love sharing my passion for history with the scouts and their leaders.

The preparation is time consuming. I routinely tour each location months in advance of the scouts and complete a great deal of research on all aspects of the site and the people who were there. I always hope to frame the historical event as a story so that the scouts truly understand what took place and why it is important for a country to always remember its history.

A number of years ago we ventured to Valley Forge to relive the experiences of the Continental Army as they struggled through the hard winter there.

Everyone knows about Valley Forge and the terrible winter the soldiers spent there as they fought for their independence from Great Britain. This miserable experience tested George Washington's leadership and each person's resolve. The fact that the army survived at all might be one reason why they were eventually able win the Revolutionary War.

It is through the most difficult trials that heroes are born.

When studying the Revolutionary War, I find it interesting to discover and research the heroes who came from other countries to help the American cause. There were many:

Thaddeus Kosciusko, for example, came from Poland. He was an engineer who designed military fortifications for the Continental Army. Today, there are two bridges in New York (one in Albany and one in New York City) named in honor of Kosciusko.

IMPOSSIBLE IS AN ILLUSION

Pierre Charles L'Enfant came from France. He served as a military engineer, spent some time as a prisoner of war, and later served on George Washington's staff. After the war, he designed the street layout in Washington, D.C. Today, Washington's busiest Metro Station is named in his honor.

Casimir Pulaski was a Polish nobleman who was a brilliant military tactician. When the first cavalry corps was established, Pulaski was put at the head of this division. As such, today he is known as "The Father of the American Cavalry." There are a host of structures and commemorations of Pulaski across the United States. Runners in the New York City Marathon cross the Pulaski Bridge as they exit Brooklyn and enter Queens at about the marathon's halfway point.

I have always loved the stories of the Marquis de Lafayette, another French nobleman who was greatly interested in helping America secure its freedom. Lafayette served with Washington and became one of his most trusted generals, confidants, and friends. A wonderful college in Easton, Pennsylvania, Lafayette College, is named for this great man.

But for our purposes today, we'll focus on a baron named Friedrich Wilhelm Ludolf Gerhard Augustin von Steuben. (And you thought I had a long name!)

Baron Von Steuben came from Prussia to help the colonists. His life story is fascinating. He had a lengthy military background and was known throughout much of Europe. He had, at one time, served with Frederick the Great. Von Steuben came to America during that long winter at Valley Forge. It was there that he gained Washington's trust, trained the soldiers, and transformed a ragtag collection of young men into an army.

I think it interesting that even George Washington, one of the greatest leaders in history, wasn't able to win the war, or even organize and train the soldiers alone, without help from so many others. Washington needed others to assist, to step-up, to join with him in his vision, and to work with him in order to win the war. Washington was a great leader, maybe the greatest ever, but one of his best strengths was his ability to foster a team. Washington was willing to accept help, and when he saw skilled individuals, he wasn't afraid to move them into positions of authority.

As I prepared to lead the Boy Scouts to Valley Forge, it was important for me to learn more about Baron von Steuben. Specifically, I wanted to find out what he did to prepare and train the soldiers so that they became a military force to be reckoned with.

The first aspect of Von Steuben's approach that caught my attention was his focus on drill and practice.

Von Steuben began his work by creating a model company. He did this by taking the very best soldiers from the rank and file. He first explained and taught his military tactics to this model company. He taught them how to maneuver and how to march as one unit. He also taught them the proper use of the musket and bayonet. The movements, the routine, was taught, reviewed, and practiced - over and over again.

Once this model company mastered the program, the rest of the army was brought into the act. It was through drill and practice, repetitive drill and practice, that the American army was made.

Drill and Practice.

Today, those words, in educational and other circles, are frowned upon. We're told not to drill. Teachers are told to let children explore and find their own learning styles. Yes, this is true even for children in the earliest grades. Educators are told that drilling or repetition is ineffective.

IMPOSSIBLE IS AN ILLUSION

And yet...

I know, through my own experiences in learning to master things such as hitting a baseball, or in learning to play the saxophone or piano, that the way to build skills is through drilling. If one wants to master a specific skill, he must repeat those actions over and over again. It is no surprise that the songs I play the best are the ones I have practiced the most.

Drill and practice works. It works absolutely.

Drill and practice is an effective tool for mastering physical skills and also memorizing important facts.

Drilling instills discipline. This is as true for learning the discipline of math facts, spelling, and the rules for excellent writing as it is for mastering the art of throwing a curve ball or playing scales, chords, and arpeggios.

Before I ever speak publically, I review my speech or presentation over and over again. That's drilling...and practicing.

Before running a marathon, a runner must go through a rigorous training program that usually lasts for at least four months. That constant running is drilling and practicing.

Now, please note, if the only way we instructed or taught new skills was through drill and practice, we would be off base. Schools would become places that are not stimulating, and we would be creating students who work only on rote memory. That isn't true learning. Learning must be more than just memorization.

So, in addition to the drilling and practicing, educators must come up with ways to add fun and allow room for creativity. Sure, a pianist needs to practice certain skills. But that player must also be permitted to play the songs he enjoys and to also create melodies, rhythms, and techniques of his own. That is where true growth takes place.

Drills instill pride. When students are at their best academically they feel better about themselves. And when students know their facts, in any subject areas, they become more confident, more willing to take risks, and through this, they can take their learning to the next level. Drilling helps set the foundation that allows for true growth.

One might imagine Von Steuben, or any person with a drill and practice approach, as a tyrant. One might picture him yelling at the men during that cold winter at Valley Forge:

"Do it again, Do it again!"

But, our dear Baron wasn't a tyrant. He actually demonstrated through his actions, manner, and his written words, that the teacher, the instructor, and even the drill sergeant must respect, and even love, each of the learners.

It's true. Baron Von Steuben felt that love was an important aspect of learning.

In his famous handbook on military matters, Von Steuben spent much of the text insisting that the key to being a successful leader is to instill love, not fear, into the soldiers. The great Prussian general sought to win over the Continental Soldiers not with humiliation, or hard discipline, but with love. He understood that at the heart of leading is understanding that the people we lead are human – that their lives matter.

I believe that people do their best when they know their teachers, their bosses, or their leaders truly care about them. When leaders bring humanity to their decision making, when they demonstrate that they can empathize, they become transformational.

IMPOSSIBLE IS AN ILLUSION

I believe this is one characteristic that separates poor leaders from good ones. I also believe that this is what separates good leaders from exceptional leaders.

Baron von Steuben's leadership was integral in developing the army that won us our independence. In a different life, in different circumstances, although some of his ideas might not be cutting edge right now, he would have also made an excellent leader today. He wouldn't be afraid to go against conventional wisdom to do what truly works. More, he knew that a loving and caring teacher is integral to the process of learning and helping his students achieve success.

The Story of a Sax

DR. PAUL SEMENDINGER

I was eight years old. A third grader. Elementary school...

We had to choose an instrument to play.

I picked the saxophone because I thought it was the coolest instrument.

* * * *

Like any third grader, I began playing with great enthusiasm, and after just a few lessons I could play numerous simple songs.

I got better and better, and the more I played, the more I enjoyed my instrument.

Eventually, I took private sax lessons at a music studio, and everybody said I was pretty good.

"That boy can play the sax," they'd say.

The saxophone is a very cool instrument.

* * * *

By seventh grade, I was the number one sax player in the elementary school band. I sat first in a long line of saxophone players – altos first, then the tenors on the stage. I was the one player who sat closest to the audience. I was the saxophone player they would see. I was proud.

But, either our school concert band was too big, or our stage was too small...

IMPOSSIBLE IS AN ILLUSION

The set-up on the stage had me sitting precariously close to the edge, and in one practice, just before a concert, I fell off the stage. The chair, my precious sax, and I – we all fell together.

The chair was fine. I was stunned, but no worse for the wear. My sax, not so much. The edge of the bell (the big round thing in the front of the saxophone) was bent.

It stayed that way for about thirty-five years.

* * * *

The first day of school as a new student in high school wasn't pleasant for me. I remember walking into the band room, sax case in hand. The upper classmen were huge. They scared me, but even more frightening was the band director. I'll never forget his opening message.

"If you are in the band," he said, "this is your life for the next few months." He went on to explain how we practiced daily, and also on weekends. He talked about marching and football games. "You'll be at every football game," he announced. Rain, snow, wind, cold…we'd be there.

All of a sudden, playing an instrument didn't seem like much fun to me. It would be a job. I wasn't ready to have a job.

That night I went home and told my parents that I didn't want to play the saxophone any longer.

They let me quit.

* * * *

DR. PAUL SEMENDINGER

It was a long separation.

* * * *

My sax and I would see each other on occasion. I'd take it out of the case, put it together, feel it in my hands, and blow out some tunes. If once I was good, I wasn't any longer.

The more time went by, the less we saw of each other. The sax now mostly lived in the attic. I wondered about selling it a few times, but I couldn't.

I thought, "Maybe someday I'll play again."

* * * *

Someday came when I was about 31 years old.

By that time I was the principal of Fieldstone Middle School in Montvale, New Jersey. In a discussion with the band director, I indicated that I knew my way around a saxophone. I stated that I probably couldn't play too well, but that I could still make it make some noise and play some easy notes. The band director was intrigued.

The next thing I knew, I had joined the seventh and eighth grade concert band.

(Originally I insisted that I join the fifth and sixth grade band as I felt beginners more accurately reflected my skills after not playing for nearly a quarter of a century. The band director wouldn't hear of it. He put me with the big kids.)

IMPOSSIBLE IS AN ILLUSION

I went to the band practices before school and relearned how to translate the notes on paper to placements of my fingers on the instrument. I learned again about slurring and tonguing notes.
I wasn't as good as these middle school kids, but they seemed to like that I was in the band, and I liked it as well. I especially enjoyed joining the band in their various concerts over the years. I got a little better over time, but I never found that old magic.

I was able to keep up with most of the songs. I was best on whole notes and quarter notes. (And no one played a rest better than me.) On the really fast or challenging parts, I just put my sax on my knee and let the kids lead the way. I never wanted to distract from their performance by hitting wrong notes.

My saxophone and I enjoyed a good nine-year run playing in that middle school band, but an elementary school was calling me…

* * * *

Now forty years old, and principal of Hawes Elementary School, in Ridgewood, I was certain my saxophone playing days were over.

I thought that I might sit in with the fifth grade band on occasion, but they were just beginners. I figured playing with them would be more of a distraction than an addition.

But then there was this thing called Dads' Night and the Dads' Night Band…

* * * *

Word got out that I could play the sax.

"Not well," I insisted… "NOT WELL!"

It mattered little. I soon became a guest member of the Dads' Night Band. These men play the music for a variety show that is somewhat akin to modern-day Vaudeville as a great way to raise funds to support two local schools.

Dads' Night is an amazing program full of dedicated fathers who freely give of their time, their energies, and their talents.

But here is the thing about the Dads' Night Band… these are not just a group of men trying to play music. These men are good. Real good. If they aren't all pros (some of them are), they could be.

And the Dads' Night Band doesn't play middle school concert music, they play rock-and-roll. They play it loud and well and good. And it's fun. Real fun.

Everyone loves the Dads' Night Band.

These dads (the most patient musicians ever), put up with my struggles, mistakes, wrong notes, and stumbles. I attend their practices. I rehearse. I spend long evenings after work jamming. We play on weekends. I get invited to practice in some private homes.

It is cool.

I've never played great music like this before.

Where I can, I play. When the songs are too challenging, I sit out. Over the years, I've even had a few simple solos. The parents and the kids seem to love that I play in the Dads' Night Band.

I love that I play.

For about five weeks each year, I get to think I'm a rock star.

IMPOSSIBLE IS AN ILLUSION

* * * *

This year, the band has given me my biggest challenge yet. They want me to play the Benny Hill theme song (also known as *Yakety Sax*) on the stage - with one of the acts.

I am a big believer in trying. I am trying. My fingers just don't move that fast.

Seeing this dilemma, one of the band leaders rewrote the sheet music, making it a lot simpler for me. Instead of playing every note, I'd just have to hit the main quarter notes, and I'd now be supported by another dad – a real saxophone player. My fingers still don't move quite fast enough.

But I am trying.

The show is in nine days. These are nine long days with many practices. I'll be playing that song in my sleep, I think.

If I can get this figured out, if I can get my fingers and my brain to work together to pull this off, I will have grown as a saxophone player tenfold in just a few weeks.

It'll be a short-lived triumph. I'll be playing on stage for only a minute or two for two shows and then it will be over. But it'll be a triumph nonetheless.

I'm not sure if I can do it, but if I can…

If I can do it, if I can play the Benny Hill Theme, I will be doing something that my ten-year-old self thought would have been a regular part of my adulthood.

DR. PAUL SEMENDINGER

The ten-year old me would be disappointed that the 47-year-old me doesn't play the sax very well. He would ask, "What happened?"

I could tell the long story to that ten-year old me, but instead, I'd like to try to make that little kid proud.

I think I can do it!

The New York City Marathon 2016

DR. PAUL SEMENDINGER

Now for a change…

This essay will be a little different than the others. It might not end up as a passage with one main theme. More, it's a stream-of-conscious recollection of my experiences at the 2016 New York City Marathon.

So much happens during the whole marathon experience that it's almost impossible to single out any one moment to define the entire experience. Instead, all that the marathon encompasses come together as small vignettes, each important but each only part of a collective whole. It is the conglomeration of these parts that make the entire marathon the awe-inspiring event that it is.

Since I wrote this passage a week after I ran, I'm sure some of the most poignant and special things that I wanted to remember had been lost among the crowds, thrills, and emotions of the day. The marathon is too encompassing for a participant to remember every important detail.

Background:

- I ran my first New York City Marathon in 2002. It was a life changing event. Absolutely. I felt the love of New York City and it carried me over the 26.2 miles. There are times when I think I still haven't come off the highs I experienced that day. It was all glory, wonder, and joy. I sometimes get teary eyed remembering that blistery cold and most wonderful day.

- Since that first marathon in 2002, I have run 19 other marathons. The race this year was my 20th marathon and my 6th in New York City.

IMPOSSIBLE IS AN ILLUSION

- I have enjoyed some wonderful marathons for many different reasons. Chicago, in 2006, was one of the best experiences. My wife and I traveled with our dear friends, Ed and Melissa Hasse, for a long weekend there. We had the best time together. I loved the city. I ran my Personal Record (PR) time in Chicago (3:26:16). I've run the Disney World Marathon twice, once as part of the Goofy Challenge. My children were much younger then... Still, I will always love using running as an excuse to visit Walt Disney World.

- I now run marathons as "excuses" to travel to see my sons at their colleges. I will always love using running as an excuse to see my sons.

- As much as I have loved many of the race venues that I have experienced, nothing compares to New York. I long to run this race every year. A part of me absolutely lives each year for the New York City Marathon. When I don't get into the race (that darn lottery is tough), my heart sinks.

Race Day – PreRace:

- For this race, it takes a marathon effort just to get to the staging area at Fort Wadsworth, Staten Island where the race eventually begins. One reason it's hard to set a PR in New York is the amount of time is takes just to travel to the start. The logistics are challenging. This year, since we were car-pooling, we left our home at 4:30 a.m. in order to get to the shuttle buses at the New Jersey Meadowlands in time. (My race start time was 10:40 a.m.)

- I don't sleep particularly well the night before a marathon. That morning I was up at 2:15 a.m. At 3:30 a.m., I went outside into the cool November air to soak in our hot tub and contemplate the day. I thought, often, of the challenge ahead and looked forward to returning to that very spot many hours later to, literally soak in the accomplishment of completing another marathon. (In those early hours, the stars were beautiful. I enjoyed the peace of watching them twinkle in the sky.)

- I was impressed with the logistics of the shuttle buses and at the start area. In previous years, these processes were less organized and it all seemed more like hopeless confusion. This year it was well organized and ran extremely smoothly. Kudos to New York Road Runners (NYRR)!

- I was surprised there was food at the starting area. I had never known that food was available at Fort Wadsworth. Previously, I just found a dry spot to hunker down and tried to stay warm (or I went to assist at the non-denominational worship tent). This year, I was thrilled to get Gatorade, two Power Bars, a bagel, and a banana. It was a regular feast! The prized items at the start were the free Dunkin Donuts knit hats. Everyone had to have one. (Me, too, but I sent mine home with a friend who checked his bag. I had already brought a knit hat with me.)

- I was also thrilled to be a leader this year at the worship tent. I find this to be an awe-inspiring, spiritual, and uplifting experience. It is great to welcome God into the marathon experience and to share His love and spirit as part of the day. This year I delivered two sermons (at two different services) and also helped with celebrating the Eucharist. The feedback from the sermons (they were based, of course, on running) was very positive. Somewhere inside of me is a preacher itching to get out.

- I was thrilled to meet Chuck Nebbia, a valued colleague, at the service tent – and I was touched that he stayed to listen to one of my sermons. After the service, I enjoyed basking in his anticipation and excitement since this was his first marathon. (We would meet again many hours later.)

IMPOSSIBLE IS AN ILLUSION

- My friend, Ed Hasse, is one of the leaders each year at the worship service. I will always value and treasure the huge smiles he wore as he watched and listened to my (hopefully inspiring) words. He would be running the race with his daughter (her first marathon) later that day. That was a very special and wonderful experience for them. I hope to one day guide my sons over the same 26.2 miles.

- Soon it became time to head for our own starting corrals. I parted with my old friends and newly-made friends. The start area of a marathon provides unbelievable opportunities for people to bond. We all know what is ahead. We're all full of nervous anticipation. We are also filled with doubt and fear. I think we appreciate the camaraderie and support - otherwise, the start of a marathon can be a very lonely experience.

- Even with the friends, new and old, the start is, at times, a lonely place.

- Before departing, I was asked by two friends to predict my finish time. I said, "4:22:00." They laughed. "Can you be more specific?" they asked. I laughed too. What a dumb answer!

- I met an older couple in line for a port-a-john. They were each well into their sixties but found marathoning late in life and loved running together. They used the marathon as a way to see the country. This couple was from the State of Washington. They had traveled over 3,000 miles to run NYC.

- And then I found myself, alone, amid thousands of others at my start corral waiting for the gates to open.

- I was very happy this year that the weather was so warm. Previous years my start experience consisted mainly of shivering. Still, there comes a point when one has to start shedding layers. This is always a challenge. "Will I need these gloves" "Will I need this sweat shirt?" "What about my hat?" (I kept my gloves, knit hat, and a long sleeve wicking shirt (which I tied around my waist). I was glad for the gloves and hat later on the course as there were times when it was quite chilly. The shirt just traveled the whole way with me. I didn't untie it until the race was over and I was on my way home. I guess I could have left it behind.

The Start:

- The corrals opened and I found a nice curb to sit on for about 20 minutes before the area got too crowded to allow for such comfort. I stood up knowing that the next time I'd sit would be many hours and many miles later.

- Soon we were walking to the start. A woman named Renee talked nervously to me. She was from Canada. People were excited. Many were jumping up and down as we made our way to the start lines. I was actually close to the front of this gigantic mass of people. I could actually see the starting line. I knew my chip time wouldn't be that different than the clock time. It's not always that way when one runs New York.

- Some people were already beginning to smell badly. It's a hazard of the sport. I hoped I wasn't one of them. But what do you expect when you cram 50,000 people together for a running event?

- I was in the "Green" corral. This staring area would run on the lower level of the Verrazano Bridge. I had never started on the lower half of the bridge.

- "God Bless America" was sung beautifully. The throngs stood at reverent attention. That was great to hear and see.

IMPOSSIBLE IS AN ILLUSION

- Soon a cannon blasted and we were off. "New York, New York" blared over the speakers. That song always hits me right in the heart. I love New York City!

The Race:

- Like all huge races, the start was slow. The climb up the Verranazo Bridge wasn't too tough. I felt good. I was able to scoot around slower runners, but didn't do much of that. The runners were orderly and calm. The atmosphere was positive.

- As a veteran of five previous New York Marathons, my excitement built as we started to descend the bridge. I relish the wall of people, the cheering, and the euphoria that first greets runners as they charge into Brooklyn.

- What a let-down! Runners coming off the lower Verrazano do not experience the initial crowds in Brooklyn. Instead it's a quiet entrance on empty lonely roads to begin the trek into this great borough. At one point, as I was descending the bridge, I heard the familiar roar of the crowds off in the distance. I was reminded of that sound as I pushed ever forward waiting for this course to merge with the other runners around Mile 3.

- I felt absolutely great the first few miles. The chill in the air on the bridge, and after, made me glad I kept the knit hat on my head.

- Mile 3 (or so) came, and with it the crowds. Euphoria! This is what I love!

- I was wearing a Superman shirt. I did not wear my name on my shirt front as in other years, but, it began almost immediately - the cheers for Superman, the cheers for me.

- I'll never be able to explain how wonderful it is to see and hear people, thousands and thousands of people, looking at me and yelling "Go Superman," "Yeah Superman," "You are Superman." I'm a far cry from Superman, a far cry, but…one tends to believe the hype after hearing it over and over.

- I AM SUPERMAN!

- One might think that interacting with the crowds would slow down a runner's time. Maybe it does, but the New York crowds fuel me. I ran right next to them (as I always do) and gave high fives, hand slaps, and felt enveloped by their love. When I felt particularly energetic, I'd yell to the crowds, "Yeah Brooklyn!" "I love Brooklyn," "Brooklyn Rules," or, simply, as loud as I could "BROOKLYN!!!!" The responses I'd get gave me extra energy to keep moving forward. I just love the crowds, the people, and the unique character of New York.

- I love the grimy, gritty, edgy, streets. I love the tough aspect of New York. It's a hard city – a tough city. I'm anything but tough, but I embrace all of this on Marathon Day.

- The miles seemed to pass more quickly than they should have. It seemed every few minutes I'd zoom through water stations and mile markers. I wasn't running particularly fast, but the race was flying by!

- In my training, I developed a plan where I ate from a Clif Builder Bar every odd numbered mile (1, 3 5, etc.), and drank Gatorade or water every even numbered mile (2, 4, 6, etc.). It helped pass the time and it gave me just the right energy. I brought two Clif Builder bars with me to eat during the marathon, but I realized at Mile 7 that I hadn't consumed anything except Gatorade at a few of the water stations. (I won't call them water stops because I grabbed the drinks and just kept going.) Realizing that I hadn't eaten, I pulled a partially melted bar out of one of my arm pockets, and took a huge bite.

- I was taking Gatorade or water at most stations. I always try to thank the volunteers there and at the aid stations. They have a huge job…and their day lasts longer than the runners'.

- I purchased a Flip Belt at the NYC Marathon Expo the day before and this item worked extremely well. The Flip Belt is sort of like a flat "fanny pack." It's a great place to store energy gels or energy bars, a cell phone, and more. It hugged my body and the items I was carrying didn't bounce or distract me at all. I highly recommend the Flip Belt.

- I had hoped to see a teacher from my school who was spectating at Mile 3 (or was it Mile 4?). I didn't see her. I tried to see another employee from work at Mile 9. I searched with every step beginning late in Mile 7 and continued through Mile 10, or so, but never found him in the crowds. (In past years I was much more able to find people I was looking for.)

- I love the motivational signs held up by the spectators. This year there seemed to be a lot of "Touch Here to Power-Up" signs. I touched a few.

- The political signs, though, were tired and distracting. The NYC Marathon is a time for the city to come together, not to be separated by politics.

- I high-fived so often with my right arm that it was starting to get tired and sore. My shoulder too. To rectify this, I ran on the left side of the road for a while, but it wasn't quite the same for whatever reason. I guess I don't give good left-handed high fives.

- When I needed to "gather" myself, I ran in the center of the road, but soon found myself drifting back to the right side...and the crowds.

- One little boy saw me and said, with reverence and awe, "Superman." His father was about to take his picture. I stopped, bent down to his level, put my arm around him, and took a photo with him. The parent thanked me. It was awesome!

- I just love New York. I love Brooklyn. The New York City Marathon is a part of me.

- I usually don't take free items from spectators, but... One man had his son on his shoulders holding a sign that read in big letters "Candy Corn." I cut way back on sweets because of some high blood sugar numbers, so I missed the joys of candy corn this autumn. I couldn't resist this offer. I stuck my hand (still in a glove) into the huge bowl that many other runners had already thrust their own hands into, grabbed, and then delightfully ate, the most delicious candy I had tasted in a long (long) time.

- More cheering. More love. More adulation. I probably loved the crowds more than they loved me, but it didn't matter. Their passion fueled me. It always does.

- Every person should experience the joy of being celebrated and encouraged and supported for hours upon hours by people they don't know and will never see again. This is one of the joys of the New York City Marathon. THANK YOU NEW YORK. I love you!

- The bands along the course were particularly great. Their energy also pushed me.

IMPOSSIBLE IS AN ILLUSION

- I try to thank all the police and fire department members lining the course. I wish I did that even more. They deserve our appreciation. They are New York's Finest!

- Brooklyn went by too quickly. I was soon at Mile 12. I saw the Pulaski Bridge ahead. That bridge would take me to Queens. And then…NO! My left foot started to hurt, badly. The last time I ran New York, I ran with a stress fracture in my right foot. (I wasn't about to stop, of course. Marathoners are crazy. It takes more than a stress fracture to stop me.) I began to wonder if I had done it again. Did I hurt myself again? I told myself that I had "only" 14 more miles to cover, that I could do it, and I'd deal with the consequences (like last time) after the race.

- I haven't run a sub-four hour marathon in many years, but I was under two hours at the half-way point (1:55:58). I was in pain, but I was darn proud of myself. It was at this point, up the incline on the Pulaski Bridge that I walked for the first time. I didn't want to waste my strength and energy on the uphill.

- I don't remember much about Queens from this race. In past years, cheers like "Queens Rules" and "QUEENS!" never got enthusiastic responses. I also needed to stay within myself. At this point, as my strides went as such: right foot (ok), left foot (PAIN), right foot (ok), left foot (PAIN), I just needed to stay focused. Still, I drifted ever right…to the crowds and their love, support, encouragement, and never dying optimism.

- The Queensboro Bridge came quicker than I could have hoped. I usually don't "feel groovy" there. This incline, to me, is the hardest of the race. Two things happened as I made my way up. First, I determined to walk again, just a little. I wanted to conserve some energy. I still had more than ten miles to go. Second, and more importantly, my left foot stopped hurting as much. (It was sometime in Manhattan, on the other side of the bridge, that I forgot all about the pain in my quest to finish).

- I ran the downhill of the bridge knowing that would help me get back some time and also because I knew, and anticipated, the special burst of euphoria that Manhattan brings.

- MANHATTAN!!!!! I love you Manhattan!!!

- This time I was on the left side of the road. Initially the crowds seemed less interested in the nameless runners and instead were looking for familiar faces among the runners. After a few minutes of a little let-down, I found the energy to embrace the throngs. The reaction was as I hoped. They returned my love. I began to shout to all the spectators, "We love you!!!" They loved me back.

- "Go Superman!"

- By Mile 18, I knew I was tiring. I pushed as hard and as far as I could, but I came to the realization that the rest of this marathon experience would be a combination of walking and running – sometimes more of the former, sometimes more of the latter – but moving, always, ever forward.

- A parent of children in my school saw me and called my name. I stopped for her to take a photo.

- When I needed to walk, I determined to walk as fast as I could. These physical and mental breaks weren't leisurely strolls.

- Soon I was on the Willis Avenue Bridge and heading into the Bronx.

IMPOSSIBLE IS AN ILLUSION

- As I walked the incline, a spectator said, "Come on Superman." I replied, "Bridges are kryptonite." This soon became a stupid theme of mine. "High miles are kryptonite," "I left my cape at home," "Next time I'm flying," and such. The laughter and smiles from the crowd though were necessary and much appreciated.

- I still pushed my tired body. I ran more slowly than before, but the miles kept passing.

- At this point, the race is as much mental as physical. I had good spirits and knew I'd finish.

- I wanted the hell to end, but I wanted to embrace New York just as much. No, I wanted it to end more.

- I also care too much about my time. I wanted to finish as fast as I could. Pride plays a role in all of this.

- Back in Manhattan, Fifth Avenue was nothing short of torture. I'd run, and walk, and push more. Maybe I was shuffling more than running now. But I was heading in the right direction.

- Why is this incline so long?

- "Go Superman!" "You got this!" ("I know.")

- Where is Central Park? When will this end? I love New York? I do, I do, I love New York!

- When will this end?

- Soon we were in the park. This is where the crowds might be their most loud, if that is possible. A runner sees a different look in the eyes of the spectators in Central Park. There is respect. Previously there may have been some reluctant admiration, but there is some doubt, if not in the spectators' eyes, at least in the runner's head. In Central Park it is different. There is no doubt that we'll finish. Those are three long final miles, but there is no doubt we'll finish.

- I stayed to the right side of the road in the park. I remember more spectators there in past years. The throngs were on the left side of the road with big groups on the right side only gathered sporadically. Yet, when they came, or, more accurately, I arrived upon them, they were enthusiastic and helped me along.

- I couldn't wait to find the summit of Cat Hill. The downward trajectory after that summit was greatly appreciated.

- And then there was Mile 25. It comes all too soon, and not soon enough. I love Mile 25 and I hate it. Another 1.2 miles is too far, and I want the experience to be over, yet…yet, I know soon, hopefully in less than ten minutes, it'll be done…and I'll want to be back, right here again, feeling these same conflicting emotions and desires.

- No, right now I just want it over.

- Central Park South brings more enthusiastic crowds. "YOU GOT THIS THING." They know it and I know it. Those last few steps when I had to gather myself to walk were even okay. I knew I'd run through to the finish once I started again.

- I am Superman!

- Columbus Circle was ahead, I was running, and I was on my way for this last final push. It was soon back into the park for the final countdown. I love this. I love all of it. I love seeing the finish, up ahead, another small incline. As it got closer, I raised my hands.

IMPOSSIBLE IS AN ILLUSION

- I was watching the clock as I approached. 4:21:45, 4:21:46, 4:21:47. I told myself to push. I remember crossing the line, and doing some type of dumb spastic celebratory dance and fist pump, at exactly 4:22:00. What were the odds of that?

- It was over. I did it again. Every time is a struggle. Every time there are periods, sometimes long periods, of doubt. But, I did it again. A young woman put the finisher's medal around my neck. I thanked her. It was all glory. It was loud. And there was honor in finishing.

- My chip time was 4:19:59. I couldn't have been happier!

- I won the New York City Marathon for the Sixth Time!

Post Race

- The post-race long march out of Central Park is one of the least enjoyable parts of the experience. I think they have us walk for 53 miles. I'm not sure exactly. It's at least that far, probably longer. We get a heavy goody bag ("How can I even carry this?"), a heat blanket, and we just keep walking and walking endlessly. A death march.

- I did get a few finisher's photos taken. I was too happy to be too upset about the long endless march out of the park.

- I actually ran into Chuck Nebbia, the teacher from my school with whom I talked at the start and who attended my sermon and motivational message. He had finished his first marathon! He was joyful. I was thrilled to see him.

- I love the free ponchos that NYRR gives out at the end (if you don't send a bag of items to the finish). That poncho is one of the greatest things ever.

- I still had to walk about twenty city blocks south to pick up a shuttle bus to the New York Waterway Ferry to take me back to New Jersey. This was amid all of the people now looking for their family member finishers. It's less than a happy place. People just want to leave – spectators and finishers alike. Evening starts creeping in. With evening comes a chill. Now there is no glory, just a slow trudge to get out.

- As I finally approached 57th Street, where I would pick up the shuttle bus, I saw it turning, ahead of me, but I was too far away. Arms full, poncho on, legs tired, I couldn't run to catch it. Darn... I was seconds away! Because I didn't want to wait on the corner for another thirty minutes, or however long it would take for the next bus to get there, I tracked the bus that I missed on my phone (thank goodness for the Flip Belt) and saw it would come back to 8th Avenue (where I was) down on 49th Street. I started rushing farther downtown as best as I could. I silently cursed the red lights. Then, as I reached 51st Street, I saw the next Ferry Shuttle bus heading toward me. It would take me over the roads I just traveled, but I didn't care. I waved my hands frantically, the bus pulled over. I boarded the bus a champion.

- I flopped into the front seat, drew a huge breath, and called my wonderful wife. She was enthusiastic and happy for me.

- A long bus ride through the crowded streets of New York later, followed by an always enjoyable ferry ride across the Hudson River to Weehawken, and it was over. My wife stood outside the car, with a "GO PAUL" sign and a bigger smile. She's the best! A hug, a kiss, and an open door...and it concluded. Much too quickly. I love Marathon Day. I love running. I love New York. I love this race.

I Cannot Wait Until Next Year!

It's the Principle

◆

I always loved planning our summer family vacations. I would pick a place for us to visit - say Williamsburg, Virginia - and then carefully examine almost every spot we could possibly visit on the way there and home.

I tried to vary the activities along the way to keep everyone's interest. For example, as I planned the trip to Williamsburg, I allotted one day to tour the Virginia Civil War sites even though I could have easily spent a day at each of the many battlefields. The Civil War sites were for me.

On the other hand, while I'm not a huge fan of amusement parks (except those that begin with the word "Disney"), we took the time to visit Busch Gardens (which turned out to be fun, even though I didn't ride on any of the roller coasters). The amusement park was for the boys.

And then, there are sites for everyone. We all enjoy fun hotels with pools. We all like spending some time at flea markets or antique malls. And we all seem to get lost in our own ways in book stores. Those are constants on every trip.

I believe that a little bit of everything makes each trip fun and special so I work hard try to find something for everyone.

When I was young, my family camped everywhere we traveled. One summer my parents packed up their van and drove us across the country. We camped in the van (a yellow van, believe it or not) most of the nights. A night in a hotel? Well, that was a treat! (And, truth be told, most often we stayed in motels, not hotels like Hilton or Marriott, instead, the places we stayed at were more like the Roadside Rest, Route 1 Lodge, or The Mad Hatter Motel.)

IMPOSSIBLE IS AN ILLUSION

I don't mind camping, occasionally, but I also can't say that I really like it. I do like the idea of sleeping in a tent under the stars and listening to nature. But the dirt and grime and the set-up and take-down, well, it's a lot of work. With camping you also have to pack a lot of gear. It's a lot less like a vacation than a stay at the Ritz-Carlton. Oh, and then there's the campground bathrooms. I don't like them. There are always big scary spiders in the bathrooms. The rest doesn't need any description. Yuck.

Let's just say that while I may enjoy a night or two in a tent every 365 days or so, an Embassy Suites is a bit easier to manage and is much more my style.

Anyway, as part of the trip to Williamsburg, I planned one night of camping with the whole family. (My wife looks forward to camping even less than I do, but, my kids love it – and that's why we do it.)

The night of sleeping in tents was to come after a day of canoeing on the Rappahannock River. This excursion was going to be a brand new family experience, and we were all looking forward to it. Everyone was excited - until we received a call that the water was too low for canoes and our planned eleven mile adventure was changed to just three miles. We were also told that because of the low water levels, they'd be substituting kayaks for canoes.

"It'll still be great!" we all exclaimed. (At least that is how I remember it.)

It turned out that the water wasn't even deep enough for the kayaks. Where there should have been "rapids," there were rock hazards. Where we should have floated smoothly, we were stuck on the rocks. The short three-mile kayak excursion became long and frustrating. Even though we were in a river (or what was left of a river), we became very hot and uncomfortable. Most often we were pushing or pulling our kayaks down the river.

At one point, the river water was deep enough to swim. We wanted to cool off and wash away the sweat, and even though we immersed ourselves in the water, there was something about the river in this area that made me feel like it wasn't the most sanitary place to swim. (I know this - they don't use chlorine in the river).

As a family, we try to make the most of things and turn disappointments into fun – and, we did. I think. But by the time we finished pushing our kayaks through three miles of river, we were over-heated, tired, and dirty (believe it or not). We were in no shape to camp. We needed air conditioning and a warm shower. We needed clean toilets, not pits and spiders.

I had my wife call to cancel our campground reservation and ask for a refund or credit. She explained that we weren't up to camping.

Instead, all she got was "attitude." On the other end of the line was a campground employee who gave short, curt, and flippant answers.

The campground person said, in short, "No refund and no credit."

We tried to reason with them, and all they said was "No refund."

We asked if they were sold out that night, presumably if they were, they may have had to turn away people for our site. In that case, we absolutely should have had to pay. They weren't booked. I asked if someone came and took the site that night if we could get a refund, they'd still be getting their money for the camp site, I reasoned. They still refused.

Since this was a campground chain, we asked for a credit for another campground in the same system. We still wanted to camp, at least I think we did, but we needed to do it another night.

The campground people said, "No."

IMPOSSIBLE IS AN ILLUSION

Trying for just some sort of an accommodation, we asked for a credit for another night at their campground – for someday in the future, even knowing the odds were that we wouldn't ever be in that area again. They still refused.

We were hot. We were tired. We were messy. It was worth losing the money to have air conditioning and a warm shower, and toilets that flush, without spiders, so we still went to a hotel.

But, I was also a bit annoyed and angry about the curt "No refund" policy. Maybe I would have more understanding if the people we talked to were at least nice, kind, sympathetic, or understanding in the conversation. They weren't. I decided I'd take up the matter once we returned home.

When we got home, I e-mailed the campground and the company's "national offices." I received long answers from both that basically said, "No refund."

They also weren't even nice about it.

So when the Visa bill came a few weeks later, and I saw I was still charged, I e-mailed again explaining why I thought their policy was flawed.

They argued, "Hotels don't let you cancel."

"Yes, they do," I said.

"No, they don't," they replied.

"Yes, they do," I said.

"No…"

"Yes..."

(You get the idea. Their intransigence brought out the six-year-old in me.)

And then I tried to explain why their approach was flawed. I offered some suggestions. I asked them to give a little bit, to go a little in the direction of making the customer feel like his concerns mattered. They basically told me that my concerns didn't matter.

Instead, the campground people seemed too cold, too calculating, and ironically, too corporate.

I didn't win the battle. I didn't win the war.

This whole affair reminded me of a basic principle – that is, we need to listen; we need to be empathetic. Sometimes we need to go out of our way to help others or show understanding. We don't have to give people what they want, but if we don't, we at least have to listen to them, pay credence to their requests, and consider their points of view. I also think, if we're going to hold a position steadfast, we need logical and cogent arguments for why we're doing that.

Answers like, "that's just the way it is," or "I said so," are often devoid of that empathic understanding – and these answers often hurt our positions rather than strengthen them.

When we lose battles, we also lose the bigger wars.

Was it worth the cost of one night's stay for the campground and the chain to lose my family as customers...maybe forever?

I understand why the campground didn't give us our money back. Still, a small token gesture such as, "If you're in the area again, please stay with us and we'll give you a discount," would have said volumes about their empathy and understanding. I would have felt they understood. I would have felt positively about that campground – and their national chain of campgrounds.

I believe that when people know that we care, they support us. We earn support when we have people's complete trust.

It's about listening. It's about taking the time to consider nuances.

It's about being empathetic.

We need to always take the time to listen and understand others, even when we disagree with them.

* * * *

(I also learned a lesson through this experience – when planning for a night of camping, be sure to schedule a museum visit early in the day. No sweat, no bugs, and a calm day all make the prospect of spending a night in a tent sound a whole lot better.)

A Bolt!

◆

DR. PAUL SEMENDINGER

I will begin this essay by stating a most obvious point:

Usain Bolt is an amazing sprinter.

As a runner who (more and more) plods through training runs and marathons, I am in awe of Usain Bolt's speed, grace, and magnificence. Bolt seems to run with no effort as he glides across the track faster than any man alive. His magnificence comes from the fact that he has dominated the sport of sprinting for over a decade.

In a wonderful passage, sportswriter Joe Posnanski explained, in part, why Usain Bolt is so mesmerizing as a runner. He states that Bolt's running is more than just, well, running. Posnanski equates watching Usian Bolt to seeing magic. When we watch a person compete at the highest level in their field, we are watching more than just a performance. We are watching something unique and special. It is difficult to attain greatness at anything. But, to become the best in the world, as Bolt has done, over three Olympics is other-worldly.

Mr. Posnanski states "All Bolt does is run - and that is good enough."

He is correct.

I was so struck by Mr. Posnanski's piece that I forwarded it to my teaching staff with the subject line, "All You Do Is Teach." I equated the work the teachers do on a daily basis to Bolt's. Teachers, I argued, have a way of creating their own magic. When a teacher brings clarity to a difficult concept, it is something special. When a child begins to understand - that's magic. It really is. As the principal, my job allows me to see outstanding teaching. I get to see the magic that teachers create on a daily basis. This magic comes from a teacher's enthusiasm, creativity, and passion for helping children learn.

IMPOSSIBLE IS AN ILLUSION

A number of the teachers responded positively to the e-mail I sent which furthered the discussions about great teaching, great running, and excellence in general.

It was in one of these discussions that something else hit me – like a Bolt.

As great as Usain Bolt is, as much as he dominates all of these running events, there is something more about him that captures my, and the public's, attention - Usain Bolt visibly and unapologetically demonstrates his love for his sport.

As someone who follows running, the contrast between Bolt and other runners is striking. Especially in competition, runners tend to have one of two facial expressions. These are either

(1) the "jelly face" of a runner trying to be relaxed as he or she pushes through the pain and exhaustion or

(2) the "steel face" of the determined warrior giving his or her all in pursuit of excellence.

These are the looks of the competitive runner. At every level.

Except… Usain Bolt.

As Usain Bolt runs, as Usain Bolt competes, as Usain Bolt battles… he smiles.

He smiles!

One only had to watch his semi-final race in the 200 meter dash during the 2016 Rio Olympics to observe this amazing fact. As Bolt was locked in an extremely close battle with his friend and number one competitor, Andre DeGrasse...as they sprinted, feverishly, to the finish, Bolt looked at DeGrasse and smiled.

He smiled! As he did this, he also pointed his finger at his friend and seemed to say, "No, no, I am the fastest."

It is one thing to smile when you play in an over-the-hill men's softball league. Sure, we're all supposed to play for fun. It's entirely different to be smiling when competing against, and defeating, the very best athletes in the world.

Yet that's what Usain Bolt does. He smiles!

A smile says a lot to me. It is that smile, that joy, that exuberance, that makes Usain Bolt special. He is more than a great athlete; he is a virtuoso who loves his craft. Usain Bolt so enjoys his profession that he smiles as he pushes his body to its limits. And I think, ultimately, that's why the world finds him so compelling.

I discussed these ideas with a teacher and then became reflective about my own practice. After all, I LOVE my job. I love inspiring teachers. I love innovation. I love creativity. I love kids. I love making children smile. I love having a happy school. I love working to create an environment where children are valued, cherished, respected... and loved. I love learning. I love seeing kids learn. I love talking with parents. I love solving dilemmas.

On many days I feel like I have the greatest job in the world. (Every day I know that I have the greatest school in the world.)

People tell me that I smile a lot. I hope I do. But more, I hope that when people see me at work, talking with children, working with teachers, instructing, supervising, conversing, helping others...that they see the same joy in me that the world sees in Usain Bolt as he runs.

IMPOSSIBLE IS AN ILLUSION

I want others to know that I am just as happy, just as thrilled in my work, as Usain Bolt is in his.

Usain Bolt strives to be the greatest sprinter in the world.

I strive to be the greatest educational leader.

Further, it is my hope that every student and every parent sees this same look of positive happy determination on the faces of all the teachers at the school. (And I know they do.)

When we enjoy giving our very best, we create an environment that allows children to be their best. If you want children to be happy at school, surround them with happy teachers.

Usain Bolt wins almost all of his races. While I'm not sure how I stack up when compared to others, I hope that my enthusiasm and my quest for excellence are reflected in the smiles that I wear each and every day.

Brooks, Yaz, and Carlton Fisk

DR. PAUL SEMENDINGER

A few weeks ago, I took out my old set of 1977 Topps baseball cards because I wanted to find a card to use for a blog post. I enjoy creating unique visuals to use on my blog (www.drpaulsem.com).

This particular card was of Thurman Munson, the Yankees All-Star catcher.

When reminiscing about those late 1970s Yankees teams, the ones that helped me fall in love with baseball, my mind often turns to Munson. Thurman was the Yankees Captain and his grit and determination helped define the team. He was the leader on the squads that won the World Series in 1977 and 1978.

When you are young, days can seem like lifetimes. In a way, every day is forever...

(One reason life passes so quickly when we mature is that we are often looking to the responsibilities of tomorrow. As adults, we have lost the fascination with our todays.)

The lifetimes of my childhood revolved around the Yankees. Thurman Munson, by definition, was a large part of my life. And Thurman Munson's tragic death on August 2, 1979, was an event that, in some way, signaled the beginning of the end of my childhood.

I was eleven years old when Thurman's plane crashed.

Before Thurman Munson died, there was a certain invincibility of baseball players in my mind. Sure, I knew that Babe Ruth was dead. And Lou Gehrig. Ty Cobb. Players like that. But they were from long ago. The players I was watching, my heroes... they couldn't die.

IMPOSSIBLE IS AN ILLUSION

I had a poster of Thurman Munson hanging in my bedroom. It was one of those old Sports Illustrated posters, with Thurman's name across the top and a large photo of him just after he smashed a line drive (presumably for a base hit). This was the first baseball poster I ever owned. Posters of Sparky Lyle, Graig Nettles, Willie Randolph, and Reggie Jackson would follow, but ol' Thurm was the first.

I still have that poster, carefully rolled up and stored in a box in my attic.

If I were a bachelor, it would probably be hanging in my living room.

But Thurman did die. I think, somehow, knowing that Thurman Munson was dead made me begin to realize that big league baseball players weren't super heroes. It made me realize that other people in my life could die, and sure enough, they did. My grandfather died a little over a month later.

I think once one realizes that death is part of life, the innocence that is at the core of childhood begins to erode. When a kid's heroes and loved ones pass, they start to consider their own mortality and begin to wonder about their own place in the world – even if they are only eleven years old.

Still, children are resilient. I didn't grow-up over night. The change wasn't that dramatic. (My parents would say that it took me a long time to grow up.)

I wasn't necessarily thinking all of this as I held that Thurman Munson card in my hand. My main thought was originally, "I need to put this card away, back in the plastic sleeve with the rest of my 1977 set."

I don't look at my old baseball cards very often. For the most part, they just sit on a shelf in a binder. Except for when I took that card out, I probably hadn't looked at any of those cards in more than a decade – or longer.

But then, there I was, flipping through the plastic pages that contained my 1977 Topps collection.

As I looked for the page to put Thurman back in place, I lingered on a few cards that I passed.

Johnny Bench caught my eye. The Graig Nettles home run leader card too. I loved Thurman, of course, but Graig Nettles was my favorite player. I noticed Steve Carlton and Rico Petrocelli. My dad always loved Rico Petrocelli. I saw Lou Piniella, Fred Stanley, and Glenn Borgmann.

Glenn Borgmann was the first Major League baseball player I ever met. He gave a talk at my father's school, and my dad took me to see him. I remember Borgmann teaching all the kids how to properly hold a baseball in order to throw it straight. I also remember getting his autograph. Yes, I still have it.

As I flipped the pages, other names passed – Rudy May, Greg Luzinski, John Stearns, Rod Carew, Al Oliver, Mike Schmidt, Tom Seaver, and John Milner. I remembered an old New York Daily News cartoon of John Milner batting with a hammer rather than a bat.

The players I lingered on weren't all superstars, but each had a story to tell.

And then, knowing I didn't have the complete set, I began to notice the gaps in a few of the sleeves – the empty places where cards didn't lie. There were only four open spots. I was four cards away from completing the set – a task I started in 1977 and obviously never quite finished.

IMPOSSIBLE IS AN ILLUSION

I wondered which cards I was missing so I looked them up:

#285 – Brooks Robinson

#434 – *Turn Back the Clock* – Carl Yastrzemski

As a child, I wasn't always the best student. I didn't always put much effort into my school work, but early on I resolved to learn how to spell Yastrzemski. There is some research that says that when kids are forced to memorize things, they don't remember them. These experts say that memorization doesn't lead to long-term memory. I don't believe it. I have never forgotten how to spell Yaz's name.

#480 – Carl Yastrzemski (*now wait a minute…*)

#640 – Carlton Fisk

An astute baseball fan might notice something peculiar about that short list above. Three of the four cards feature Red Sox players.

I was a Yankees fan. The Red Sox were our arch rivals. Yaz and Fisk were two of the Red Sox's greatest players. The reader, right now, might be jumping to the wrong conclusion. It does seem awful suspicious that most of the cards I was missing were of Red Sox stars.

I looked up the cards on eBay, and seeing their likenesses realized that at one point, a long time ago, I had owned all four of those cards. I knew if I looked hard enough in my boxes of old cards in the attic, that I actually might be able to find the cards. I had a hunch where they might be.

This might sound strange, but the fact that they were not with my collection in these sheets, made me proud of my ten-year old self.

There is one part of this story that I haven't shared. My father is a Red Sox fan. A die-hard Red Sox fan. Even today, he can rattle off the Red Sox line-ups from the 1940s and 1950s. And, of course, my dad loves Ted Williams. Theodore Samuel Williams. The Splendid Splinter. Teddy Ballgame.

I realized that most of the cards I was missing, the Red Sox at least, were ones that I had given, as a kid, to my father. Those cards became part of his collection. In my eyes, Carl Yastrzemski was the closest player I ever saw to Ted Williams. They were both Red Sox. They both played left field. They both batted left-handed. They were both superstars. In fact, in a way that only a kid's brain works, I may have thought, at least for a time, that they were the same person.

Realizing that my set was incomplete without those four cards, I resolved to purchase them. eBay can be a wonderful thing. A few "Buy It Now's" later and four cards from my childhood were instantly on their way to my home.

I didn't order cards that were in mint or even excellent condition. In fact, I got the cheapest ones I could find. After all, these cards would be joining the ones I played with as a child. There isn't a mint card in the set. Each has flaws – small bends, rounded corners, maybe a frayed edge. Each of those cards was touched probably hundreds, if not thousands, of times. They were laid out on imaginary diamonds and stacked in fictional batting orders. They were part of original games I invented as a child. I read those cards time and again and studied the statistics. Adding mint cards to this collection would just be wrong.

One of the two Carl Yastrzemski cards I ordered was marked down because it had some writing on the reverse side. I thought that made the card perfect when I ordered it. It'll fit right in with my collection.

IMPOSSIBLE IS AN ILLUSION

There is something about items that are loved, and worn, that make them special.

There is also something about items, like baseball cards, that can instantly bring us back to the past – and that can be a wonderful thing. Through my baseball cards, I was able to remember parts of my childhood – the players and the real-life people who were my heroes. I also got to see my ten-year-old self again and be a little bit proud of who I was.

I was able to purchase all four of the cards, four Hall-of-Famers no less, for less than eight dollars in total. That seemed to be a bargain for cards that are almost 40 years old.

One might say that those old cards have very little value.

I'd have to disagree.

Hiroshima
July 5, 2012

In 2012, I embarked on a two-week educator's tour of Japan. It was an amazing experience and I was fortunate to be able to bring along Ryan, my eighteen-year-old son, who would soon be heading off to Lafayette College. I treasure the moments that we experienced together.

Each day in Japan was filled with wonder and provided an opportunity to learn and grow. The trip left an indelible imprint upon my soul.

I hope to someday have the opportunity to experience Japan again.

The experiences, however, were not necessarily all happy ones.

One of the difficult days was July 4, 2012, when we visited Hiroshima - one of the cities decimated by the atomic bombs dropped by the United States to end the Second World War. At Hiroshima we listened to a lecture from a survivor of the 1945 bombing, we walked through the Peace Park, and toured the Peace Memorial Museum. We also stood humbly across the river from the Hiroshima Peace Memorial, also known as the A-Bomb Dome. This was the only building to remain standing in the immediate blast area of the bomb.

The exhibits and the lecture were haunting. They brought life and reality to an important historical event.

I was amazed that there was little to no anti-American sentiment in any of these venues. More, it was all about peace.

I remember feeling that day that I wished there was more love and understanding in the world…

* * * *

IMPOSSIBLE IS AN ILLUSION

I tried to run each morning on the trip. I believe that taking the time to experience new places by foot allows people to better understand what is around them. It's good to get away from the tour bus and the scheduled sights and to just see what you can learn on your own.

I did a lot of running in Japan. I saw a great deal more because I ventured out.

On the morning of July 5, the day after our tour of Hiroshima, I was enjoying a long run through the city with a member of our tour group. After about forty minutes, my running partner turned to go back to the hotel, but I continued because I needed to experience the Hiroshima Peace Park one more time – this time running in solitude.

The mist of the morning turned to a light drizzle, and several times as I jogged over the asphalt paths that circled the park, I was moved to pray.

I ran around the A-Bomb Dome deeply thinking about my experiences in Japan. I contemplated world history, war, and also truly thought about love and redemption and hope...

As I returned to the front of the park, ready to head back to our hotel, I noticed a group of junior high students standing on some steps the near the eternal flame.

They were singing.

By now it was raining a bit harder and the smart thing to do would have been to rush back to the hotel, but I was transfixed.

It was beautiful. As they stood, in the rain, their melodious voices filled the air with a soft yet powerful sound.

These Japanese children were singing in the early hours not for anyone, but for everyone. The park was mainly empty. It was that early. And it was raining...

I stayed to listen. I may have been the only one.

After a few minutes, a woman approached me. She was either a teacher from the school or a parent of one of the singing children. She didn't speak much English, and I don't speak Japanese, but we were able to communicate. She explained that these were students from Tokyo.

"Are they singing about peace?" I asked.

She said, "Yes."

When their song ended, they turned to the monument and eternal flame, bowed, and said some words. The woman then asked me to talk to the students. I initially thought of declining, but I knew that I should say something to them. I just didn't know what...

We slowly walked toward the students, the woman asked for their attention, and then she turned to me. Standing, wet, in my running shorts and shirt, I must have made a peculiar sight. The students afforded me more respect than I deserved. Eyes upon me, they waited for my words.

"Ohayou Gozaimasu." I said. (I learned a little Japanese for the trip and this was the formal way to give a morning greeting.)

The students replied, smiling. (It may have been that my Japanese wasn't so good.)

"I am from America." (They all laughed; after all, this was pretty obvious.)

IMPOSSIBLE IS AN ILLUSION

"I am from a group of teachers and principals. We are touring Japanese schools. We will visit a junior high school in Hiroshima today. We visited schools in Toyko and will see Kyoto and Toyama also. Thank you for your singing today. It was beautiful. You warmed my heart and touched my soul. Thank you so very much."

This was but a small moment in life, a few short minutes. I talked for only 30 seconds, if that, but felt as if I was talking to the world.

I do not know if the students understood my words, but they did understand when I touched my heart and bowed toward them. They understood my smile. They understood that we are all people, together.

I waved to them. They waved back, saying "goodbye" and "thank you."

I turned and began my solitary run back to the hotel.

* * * *

If life is made up of small moments that mean everything, this was one of those moments.

I may not have made any sense to those children, but they made a difference to me.

Detour

Boy oh boy, you'd think the six-mile drive from my home in Wyckoff to little ol' Hawes Elementary School in Ridgewood would be nice and quick and easy. The last few weeks it's been anything but. I think someone decided to fix every road I drive on, but not at the same time. This has meant that each day a different road has been closed. It's now become a game... "If they close Street A, what's the next quickest way to get to Point B?"

Despite my complaining, I love driving the unique roads of Bergen County, New Jersey. For a few summers when I was in college, I drove an auto parts truck for dealer in Ridgewood known as Fairway Dodge. I would load my van in the morning and depart for a day of delivering new fenders, headlights, taillights, side panels, and other components. It was just me and the roads. Now that was a job with freedom!

Through that job I learned the nuances of every road, avenue, street, boulevard, and highway in northern New Jersey. For years after I'd amaze people if we'd drive to random places by saying things like, "You know, there's a Sunoco Station three blocks up on the left." I knew every gas station and every repair shop. I also knew where every 7/11 was. (I was a big fan of the Slurpee - especially on hot days. Those vans didn't have air conditioning.)

I loved working over the summers at Fairway Dodge. That is until they didn't have a driving job to offer me and instead said, "We'll hire you to do our inventory." Inventory – for an entire summer! It was torture. ("Three thousand two hundred thirty-three left front headlight bulbs, three thousand two hundred thirty-four left front headlight bulbs, three thousand two hundred thirty-five left front headlight bulbs...") I never want to count anything in bulk again.

Of course, I also missed the freedom the roads and highways offered me.

IMPOSSIBLE IS AN ILLUSION

I was remembering my days as parts driver as I was struggling through the recent detours that keep confronting me on my way to work. I'm a guy who gets pretty set in routines. These detours have become quite frustrating. As I stumble upon them each morning I grumble, "Uggg, I have stuff to do! I'd rather not be driving on all these different roads right now!"

But today, as I pulled out of yet another detour, I ended up right in front of one of the most wonderful little places in the Whole Wide World…Van Dyk's Ice Cream! Of course, I know where Van Dyk's Ice Cream is. I just didn't expect this one little twisting side street to lead right to what one might call Ice Cream Heaven.

There are few things in this word better than Peppermint Stick ice cream (with chocolate sprinkles) from Van Dyk's. Yum! Of course, it was early in the morning and they were closed, but I resolved at that moment that I was going to treat myself to a delicious snack on my way home from work.

If not for the detour, I wouldn't have thought about getting ice cream. It was a fortuitous surprise.

And it made me think…

Sometimes the road blocks and the detours in our lives lead us to good, happy, or unexpected discoveries. Every road block doesn't lead to misfortune. Sometimes the detours in our lives bring us the most unexpected fortune or good luck.

When we are faced with challenges, we can look upon them as reasons that we can't succeed - or we can see them as opportunities.

Too often we focus on the problems we encounter rather than the chances and hopes that the problems can bring.

When we fail, it is often because we focus too much on the pain, struggle, or difficulty of the moment. Conversely, when we succeed, it is because we keep our eyes firmly on the goals that lie ahead in spite of the challenges, road blocks, and detours. And again, sometimes, those challenges lead us to new ideas, discoveries, and opportunities.

The path to success is never straight. But the detours we face can open up new and exciting opportunities. (Like finding delicious ice cream.)

We all have to take detours. It is what we take out of them that really counts.

* * * *

(I hope they close a street and I end up near Kinchley's Pizza real soon.)

The Messages We Send

◆

DR. PAUL SEMENDINGER

Last Saturday I went out for a long run. It's one of the pleasures of spring time - getting outside in the warm air and enjoying the struggle of covering mile after mile after mile on my feet.

As I ran, I started to notice something very interesting - things that we most often take little notice of - traffic signs.

As a society we seem to have a fascination with traffic signs or at least feel the need to put them all over the place. Once I noticed how many there were, I couldn't help but be amazed. Traffic signs are literally everywhere.

The next day I decided to do an experiment. I determined to try to count all the street signs I encountered on my typical ride home from work.

Let's first frame this properly. I live in New Jersey. My commute home takes me through parts of four little towns, but in total, it's just a six-mile ride.

Six miles. It usually takes me less than fifteen minutes to make this commute door to door.

Care to guess how many traffic signs I saw over that short distance?

Think about it.

Take a wild guess.

Come on, it'll be fun.

In total, I counted no fewer than 400 traffic signs. (Take a moment and let's say this together, slowly, "Four hundred traffic signs"). And those were just the ones I was able to count from the driver's seat; I

IMPOSSIBLE IS AN ILLUSION

am certain there are more. After all, I had to keep my eyes on the road. A few times, it actually got somewhat dangerous trying to count all the signs and drive safely – there were that many of them. And this does not even include street signs (Grove Street, Ackerman Avenue, etc.) I only counted traffic signs.

That's a lot of signs. We seem to be told what to do every few feet. Literally, every time we turn around (if we're allowed to turn around), there is a street sign.

And we keep adding more.

For example, at one time, it was sufficient to have a stop sign or a traffic light. People seemed to handle that well. But now have signs that tell us that signs are coming. "STOP AHEAD" is an example, but there are plenty of others.

It used to be that people were smart enough, or aware enough, to know that when roads end or there is intersection, they should stop. No longer. People now need to be warned in advance, "Hey, up ahead you're going to see a STOP sign."

Pretty soon we're going to have signs telling us that a warning sign is approaching.

"STOP AHEAD SIGN AHEAD"

We also seem to have more and more words painted on the streets. Up until a few years ago, these read from top to bottom as such:

NO
PARKING
ZONE

For some reason, this must have confused too many people. Now the writing is backwards to seemingly make it clearer:

ZONE
PARKING
NO

Does any of this make any sense?

In addition to be inundated by signs of various shapes, colors, messages, and meanings, I also noticed that we are constantly being told what we cannot do.

The traffic signs on our roads are very negative in nature. They are demanding. They are not friendly. Wonder why so many people are cranky? Maybe they are just tired of being scolded every time they drive somewhere.

The following are just a few of the negatively worded signs that I see on my daily drive:

STOP

NO PARKING

NO STOPPING

NO STANDING

NO STOPPING OR STANDING

DO NOT ENTER

TOW AWAY ZONE

IMPOSSIBLE IS AN ILLUSION

NO TRESPASSING

NO RIGHT TURN

NO LEFT TURN

NO TURN ON RED

NO U TURN

DO NOT BLOCK DRIVEWAY

DO NOT LITTER

NO DOGS

NO OUTLET

In addition to all of this, we are told that certain areas are "HANDS FREE ZONES," to "WATCH OUT FOR CHILDREN," and to "YIELD."

(The signs always YELL at us in CAPITAL LETTERS.)

We're constantly reminded of the SPEED LIMIT and told all about SCHOOL ZONES, FIRE ZONES, FALLING ROCK ZONES, ONE WAY streets, DETOURS, and DEAD ENDS.

There are SCHOOL CROSSINGS, PEDESTRIAN CROSSINGS, and DEER CROSSINGS.

One encounters BUS STOPS and RAILROADS.

We're told we can EXIT ONLY or ENTRANCE ONLY. I am amazed that we even know if we're coming or going.

DR. PAUL SEMENDINGER

Sometimes, maybe in an effort to not use so many negative words, we have symbols with lines drawn through them. It's just a different way to say NO!

We now have blinking STOP signs. We also have signs that flash our speed. More and more there are blinking lights all over the place. People will soon be crashing their cars because of the vertigo these flashing warning signs create.

No wonder people are tired after a drive. They leave their car after being yelled at constantly by the prolific signs they encounter. Everywhere they look, they see negativity. Loud negativity.

BEWARE OF DOG

CURB YOUR DOG

DO NOT LITTER

PRIVATE PROPERTY

PRIVATE DRIVE

HIDDEN DRIVEWAY

SLOW DOWN

GET OFF THE LAWN

It gets to be a lot.

It is a lot.

IMPOSSIBLE IS AN ILLUSION

And all of this made me think, "What are the messages we give on a daily basis?" Do we look at children and say "NO, NO, NO, NO, NO, NO, NO…" like society says to us?

Do children walk in a school and see the adults as human signs spewing negative thoughts, rules, and prohibitions?

The messages we send on the roads are powerful. The signs I encounter say, very clearly, "Drivers, we have no faith or confidence in any of you." Society thinks that without the signs we wouldn't know when to speed up, slow down, or stop. The signs give the message that without them life would just be a giant car pile-up.

We are so fascinated with signs that tell us what we can't do, that we have literally changed the landscape…for the worse.

There is a section of my hometown, Wyckoff, called The Ravine. It is a very pretty spot with a picturesque brook, tall trees, and all sorts of foliage. To discourage or eliminate littering there, the local township has posted NO LITTERING signs, seemingly every few feet. Did they ever stop to think that the signs they placed are a form of aesthetic litter?

When there are too many rules, people become immune to them. When we scold or yell or complain too much, nobody hears us.

When there are too many signs, people start to ignore them.

I think this is why we have signs that warn of upcoming signs. There are so many signs that in order to drive safely and make it home alive, people have to disregard almost all of them. Our brains have made us, as drivers, immune to the signs.

Again, though, all of this makes me think of the messages that we, as educators, give to children.

Are we always telling them to SIT UP and PAY ATTENTION?

Think about the words that we utter each day:

TAKE OUT YOUR WRITER'S NOTEBOOK.

PUT YOUR PENCILS DOWN.

GO TO THE COMPUTER.

WALK.

SLOW DOWN.

NO TALKING.

LISTEN.

GET OUT YOUR HOMEWORK.

NO. (We say NO, a lot.)

TURN TO PAGE 54.

GET READY FOR MUSIC CLASS.

NO, YOU CAN'T EAT YOUR SNACK RIGHT NOW.

PAY ATTENTION.

SIT DOWN.

STAND UP.

IMPOSSIBLE IS AN ILLUSION

Have we become traffic signs? Do we have so many rules and expectations that kids, for their very existence, start to ignore the words we say just as we ignore the traffic signs?

I don't have an answer to this.

Kids need rules. Schools must have expectations. There must be a standard of behavior that is acceptable.

But what are the messages we send?

Are the messages we send ones that build children up, or are they ones that make it impossible for children to manage themselves because they are always being told, as we are when we drive, what they can't do?

Would drivers figure out how to safely navigate the roads without so many signs?

Would children do better also without constant reminders?

I don't know if there is ONE WAY to determine the answer.

But I do think it is something that we should SLOW DOWN, YIELD, and STOP to think about.

This is Not about Running

DR. PAUL SEMENDINGER

*T*his passage is NOT about running. It looks like it's about running, but it's not about running. You might think, initially, that it's about running, but you would be wrong. It's not about running.

I like to run. Well, that's not true. I often hate running. I often don't want to run. Running is hard. Running hurts. Running is a pain. Watching TV is easier. Reading is easier. Sleeping is easier. Eating candy is easier. Eating pizza is always better than running. A lot of things are better than running. I don't like running.

Well, that's not really true. In spite of the above, I love to run. There are times when running helps me relieve stress, angst, and frustration. Running makes me feel energized. Running makes me feel strong. Sometimes I think I'm Rocky Balboa when I run. (Should I have just admitted that?)

I always feel accomplished when I finish a run. Running can be great!

Running *is* great!

Well, it's apparent that I have mixed feelings about running, but, in the end, on most days I find myself running.

Most of my running is completed early in the morning inside my house on a treadmill. I love my treadmill (except when I hate it).

I like running outside ONLY in the spring and summer when the weather is warm and when it is daylight. You see, while I'm not afraid of the dark, there are a lot of things that scare me about running outside in the dark. These include dogs, deer, raccoons, and skunks. I am afraid of foxes and wolves. I am afraid of porcupines. I am afraid of potholes, rocks, sticks, curbs, gravel, ice, bottles (broken or otherwise), cars, and trucks. I am afraid of robbers and muggers and

IMPOSSIBLE IS AN ILLUSION

other bad guys. I am afraid of loose kangaroos. (Seriously, once a deer came out of the woods hopping in such a manner that I could have sworn it was a kangaroo. Scared. Me. To. Death.) None of those things scare me when I run in the light.

Well, dogs scare me. Dogs always scare me. (Robbers and bad guys too.)

Oh, and I hate the cold. When I run, I like to put on a shirt, shorts, socks, and sneakers. When I run, I like to put on things that begin with the letter "S." I don't like to wear sweatshirts, ski hats, or scarves. (Wait.) I also don't like to have to wear mittens, gloves, coats, jackets, and hoods. (That's better.)

I don't like leaving my warm house and feeling the deep chill of autumn or the bitter cold of winter. Heading out to run and being greeted by the immediate cold air is terrible. I avoid it at all costs. That's why I own a treadmill.

Jumping on my treadmill in any weather, day or night, solves all these issues. I've never been attacked by a stuffed animal.

Stuffed animals, though, have cheered me in imaginary races. This is true. I once decided that the best way to train for a marathon was to run a marathon, only it was winter. I wasn't going to run outside in the cold for four plus hours. As such, I set out to run the marathon on my treadmill. My young sons were excited by this. Knowing that I am energized by crowds at marathons, they lined up their stuffed animals to cheer me through the 26.2 miles. My sons even made me a race number that I proudly wore as I completed this singular accomplishment.

I love my treadmill... but, about seven weeks ago my treadmill broke. I cracked the frame. This happens at times in my house because I run on my treadmill...a lot. (I've since run a few other marathons on my treadmill(s). Not only is that crazy, it also helps the treadmill break.) And when my treadmill breaks, I know that it takes at least a month before all the red tape of my extended warranty is worked through and I end up either with a repair or a new treadmill.

When the treadmill breaks, I usually go to my local gym (New York Sports Club) and sign up for the one month trial membership. (Customers can sign up for this membership once every 12 months. It costs $30.00. I know a lot about NYSC's One Month Trial Membership.)

A few weeks ago my trial membership ended. There are no other local gyms that have a one month program like NYSC.

My warranty company is sending me a brand new treadmill, but it has not arrived yet.

I have no treadmill. I also don't have a gym membership. I need to run.

There is only one place to run.

Outside.

Have I shared that I hate the cold and that I am afraid of the dark?

* * * *

A few weeks ago, I had to convince myself to begin running outside in the cold and dark. This was a huge paradigm shift for me. A *huge* paradigm shift. It takes a lot to get me to put on layers of clothes and head out of my house into the dark morning outside.

IMPOSSIBLE IS AN ILLUSION

I have now been running outside in the cold and dark on most mornings.

I knew I could find every reason to hate it, but instead I set my mind to embrace the dark and chilly air.

I dare say, I have, reluctantly at first… enjoyed it.

It is kind of fun not being able to see too far ahead of myself when I run. I've been wearing one of those headlamp flashlights to help light the way. I probably look foolish, but it's a novelty. Since it's dark and I really can't see, I figure it makes no sense to completely shut out the rest of my senses, so I have not been bringing my iPod. The only music is what is playing in my head (most often the *Rocky* theme). The only sounds are my breathing.

It's different. It's not easy. I still don't like the first cold mile or so, but I find I warm up well enough. It's kind of neat to see the steam of my breath as I run – and not be cold.

I don't see too many people, but the ones I encounter are always friendly. They smile at me. (It is possible that these people are smiling only because they are about to laugh at "Stupid Headlamp Guy.") I have not been attacked by dogs, or wolves, or even kangaroos. (Yet.)

Things change. I am running outside, not inside, but in the end, I'm still doing the same thing – I'm running. It's a little different, it's not what it usually is, but I'm still running.

It's a challenge. It's a little bit scary. But it's good. I like it.

I'm running.

DR. PAUL SEMENDINGER

* * * *

Education these last few years has become more of a challenge.

It seems every year there is a new requirement, mandate, or policy. It seems every year they give these acronyms: TPES, NJASK, SLO, CCCS, NCLB, SGP, QSAC, PARCC, MAP, WTW, EE4NJ...

And then there are new academic programs and computer programs. We attend programs to learn about programs. These all get fancy names: Skyward, Blackboard, Race to the Top, Link-It, Learnia, OASYS, Rosetta Stone, FOSS, enVision...

All these things are new. All these things can be frustrating. All these things can be scary.

All of these things are like running outside in the cold and dark. They have the potential to break us down. They have the potential to make us want to stay inside our own little shell. They are hard. They aren't the way we used to do it.

They are also paradigm shifts.

But in the end, no matter how many alphabet letters and acronyms there are, no matter how many programs we adopt... in the end, each day a bunch of kids come to our classrooms and look for us to teach them.

In the end, it's just the teacher and the kids. In the end, children just want to be taught.

The answer to all of this is to just... teach them.

Teaching should be the real focus. Teachers should invest their best energies in the art of what they do best – teaching.

IMPOSSIBLE IS AN ILLUSION

The other stuff just distracts from the process of working with and helping kids. The other stuff is often just noise.

(*Note – This passage was written about five years ago. Many of those new "State-of-the-Art" innovations and programs have come... and gone. In the end, they really were just distractions.*)

* * * *

When I run outside, I could focus on what I hate and what I am scared of. I decided against that so I can make the most of my runs. I don't let the baggage weigh me down. When I focus just on my running, all is good. (The other stuff is still there – dark, cold, dogs – but they aren't my focus.)

When you're teaching, you can focus on all of the "other" stuff and it might weigh you down. Instead, focus on what's good and you'll feel better. When you focus on teaching – because that's what you do – all will be good. The other stuff is still there, but those things shouldn't be the focus.

Just teach and all will be well.

* * * *

I'm heading outside now for a run.

Dr. Sem's Guide to Fitness

Yes, this is a free feature – a book within a book. People pay big money for fitness guides. Every book store has shelves crammed full of books that teach people how to get into shape each boasting the best methods and theories, and the newer the books are, the better their shelf position.

The discount shelves, on the other hand, are full of last year's latest fitness theories.

Some prolific authors can be found on both shelves. That's impressive. "Listen to me," those books seem to say, "I have the most recently out-of-date fitness model and the newest state-of-the-art approach. Trust me. I know what I'm talking about."

One of these days I might write a book about fitness. (It'll be a best seller, I can guarantee that.) But since that's a day off in the future, this passage will have to suffice. (Please buy my book when it is published.)

My fitness book will never go out-of-date because my fitness plan is timeless.

Despite what most people think, knowing how to get in shape is not difficult. Everyone already knows the answer: You just have to do it.

Everything about getting into shape flows from one simple fact. It actually flows from one simple word. The *Dr. Sem Guide to Fitness* can be summarized with that one word:

Motivation.

It's all about motivation.

IMPOSSIBLE IS AN ILLUSION

And it really is that simple.

If a person is motivated, he or she will get the job done. If the motivation is not there, all sorts of excuses will get in the way and serve as distracters to getting into shape.

Now the reader might be saying, "No, it's more than that. You need to eat right. You need to do certain exercises. You need certain equipment. And more."

No, it's really just about motivation.

That's why my fitness plan will never go out of style. All of the other things are very important, but they all only come after a person is motivated to get fit.

A motivated person will eat right. A motivated person will do certain exercises. A motivated person will find or save enough money to get the right clothes or equipment. But without motivation, all the plans, all the diets, all the programs, all the exercises, and all the equipment are meaningless. None of those things matter if the person isn't motivated enough to actually get fit.

Let me take a step back now because I think this important:

I exercise every day. Every single day. (I keep track of this, which is something I'll get to in a bit.) I force myself, every single day, to exercise in one way or another. I run numerous races every year including marathons. I also play competitive (old man) men's softball, I backpack and hike, and more. I'm active. Very active.

But I'm not as fit as I can be or should be. It's a lifelong process and I'm not "there" yet. (And "there" seems awfully far away.)

I have also fallen into the trap of "I exercise a lot so I can do anything or eat anything." I learned that those are fallacies that get in the way of true fitness.

For the last few years, my doctor has been concerned about my blood sugar levels. Each year the number goes up a little bit more. At my last check-up, a few months ago, I was extremely close to pre-diabetic levels. By some measurements, I am in the pre-diabetic range. I'm not happy about this.

I don't eat all that well. I love pizza. I could eat pizza every day. Pasta is my best friend. I like white pasta, white bread, and white rice. Candy is delicious. Ice cream is wonderful. My favorite drink is sweetened iced tea. I think McDonald's hamburgers are wonderful. French fries too. Burger King added mozzarella sticks to their menu. Yum! And I love soda. I think cola is one of the most refreshing treats in life. I absolutely love cola.

For years I ate whatever I wanted. Sure, I tried to be smart, and I often was, but my habits were part of me. I always reasoned that my running kept all the bad food in check. I ran off the pounds. I ran off the sugar. I figured a guy who was as active as me, a guy who runs marathons, couldn't possibly be a diabetic.

But I was wrong.

When the blood sugar number came after my last check-up, I was humbled...and scared. My plan had failed me. I was on my way to diabetes. (I might still be on that path.) If I wasn't officially a pre-diabetic, I was certainly a pre-pre-diabetic.

I knew I had to change some things in my diet and my approach.

And I did.

IMPOSSIBLE IS AN ILLUSION

I did this because I was motivated.

I read articles on diabetes and pre-diabetes. I took out books from the library. I visited a nutritionist. I learned a lot. But most of what I learned, I pretty much already knew.

As, I suspect, you already know.

I had to change my eating habits (although I still don't eat enough vegetables). I had to give up a lot of what I love. I had to cut back on almost everything sugar-based. Most of all, I learned to force myself to limit my intake of carbohydrates. Carbs were killing me. I had to have a separation from the foods I love the most.

I have lost about twenty pounds and reduced my blood sugar levels out of the very dangerous range. I'm not out of the woods, and I never will be, but I am on the right track.

Even after losing the twenty pounds, I still don't have six-pack abs. I lift weights numerous times each week, yet my physique is a far cry from Rocky Balboa. People don't see me and say, "Wow, that guy is in shape," or "That guy is huge." (They do say, "Hey, that guy is going bald.")

How was I able to lose twenty pounds?

How was I able to change my eating habits to the "Better, but Far-From-Perfect" category?

How am I able to exercise every day?

Motivation.

I believe motivation comes from within. If we want something badly enough, we'll do whatever it takes to get it.

I want to be in good shape. I don't want to be a diabetic (if I can help it). I want to play great softball. I want to run a hundred more marathons. I want to live forever.

That type of motivation.

Motivation makes it possible for me to make critical decisions and sacrifices and force myself to do what is necessary to be my best self.

People sometimes tell me that they'd like to be in better shape, but they don't have the time. I think we all can make the time. We just have to make the decision that getting into shape is our goal. Often people who don't work out just value other things ahead of exercise.

The time one spends scrolling through the news in bed or on the couch could, instead, be spent exercising.

The time one spends on line at the coffee chain each morning, instead, could be spent exercising.

For many people, television comes at the expense of exercise.

Surfing the net comes at the expense of exercise.

Sleeping often comes instead of exercise.

There are many things people do instead of exercising. The time to do what is necessary to get into shape is there; most people just choose to use it for other things.

For me, the trade off was easy. I don't watch much television. Most of the shows I do watch, I enjoy while exercising. I get up at 4:00 a.m. and I find that most often I don't miss the sleep, although I do go to bed early...usually around 9:30 p.m.

IMPOSSIBLE IS AN ILLUSION

Why do I do this? Because I am motivated to.

That's the simple answer.

Motivation is the key.

In regard to special diets, special exercise routines, and special equipment – my answer is probably what the reader expects. We all know how to eat correctly. We know which foods are healthy and which aren't. We know we should eat junk food in moderation, or not at all. Soda isn't good for us. We should reduce our sugar intake. Too many carbs aren't good. We need to eat fruits and vegetables. We know what to do. If we're motivated enough, we will eat right.

My path toward diabetes has forced me to eat better. I visit my old food friends only occasionally. I really don't have a choice.

I also don't believe there are any magic workouts or magic exercise machines. Every workout works. Every machine works. Put in the time, put in the effort, doing any exercise - and you'll get into shape.

Getting in shape requires only time, effort, and consistency. That's all. A person must commit to it.

As I mentioned above, one way that I force myself to be accountable is that I keep track of every exercise. I write down every effort on a calendar. This keeps me "honest." I abhor missing days. As such, I'm motivated to never skip or see a blank day on my calendar. I chart my runs. I look for ways to improve and I keep at it.

I don't have to make a decision each day to exercise. I made that decision a long time ago. I want my future self to be pleased with the person I am today.

DR. PAUL SEMENDINGER

I'm hoping to live to have a vigorous old age because I gave the efforts today to work hard and eat right.

I think the sacrifices are worth it.

Old Peanuts and Today

DR. PAUL SEMENDINGER

Of all the comic strips ever created, the *Peanuts* strip created by Charles Schulz is undoubtedly my favorite. (*Calvin and Hobbes* would be a close second.)

In the early 2000s, a number of book companies committed to republishing every single *Peanuts* strip in chronological order – a total of nearly 18,000 strips. These anthologies came in many different shapes and formats.

I considered the idea of buying every volume, so that I could own every single *Peanuts* strip, but then I realized that I would need an addition on my house to store them all. ("Honey, it seemed like a good idea at the time…")

So instead I started doing the next best thing – I have been taking the published volumes out of the library. I have embarked on a journey to explore the entire *Peanuts* phenomenon. There are probably about a million things that would be a better use of my time; nonetheless, this is an interesting project and a fun diversion from some of my more serious work.

It has been fun to watch the characters develop and change over time. Schroeder, for example, began his comic life as a baby – much younger than Charlie Brown and his other friends. But within a few years, Schroeder somehow aged, while the others did not. Lucy's "career" also began as a little child. She had haunting wide eyes (some call this the "Bug-Eyed Lucy" stage). I wonder how long it was before someone said to Mr. Schulz, "Hey Charles, nice comic, but that Lucy character – she's scary."

I have also been amazed by the number of characters previously unknown to me who have popped up here and there in the *Peanuts* cartoon. Over the years, characters were shuffled in and out, many

IMPOSSIBLE IS AN ILLUSION

never to return. It may come as a shock, but Snoopy had seven siblings who have appeared in the comic strips.

It seems that Charles Schulz was always experimenting with the strip, always looking for a new approach and a unique way to connect with his audience. The fact that Schulz was so creative and willing to experiment, I think, is one reason the strip lasted for over fifty years and also why it was so endearing – and as we see now, timeless.

This is one of the characteristics of success – a willingness to step out of a comfort zone and seek to improve. While I love the comic, as I read through the entire treasury I have found that there were many individual strips that just didn't have much to them. While there are many funny strips, some just seem to fall flat.

Believe it or not, I think this may have been another reason for the success of the *Peanuts* strip. We fail sometimes. Charles Schulz was no different. No writer or cartoonist is perfect.

One early *Peanuts* strip that I discovered and greatly enjoyed involved Charlie Brown as a contestant in a spelling bee. Charlie was certain he would do well. The first word he was asked to spell was "maze." Charlie, who was always thinking about baseball, thought of the "Say Hey Kid," the centerfielder for the New York and San Francisco Giants in the 1950s and 1960s and spelled his answer "Mays" (Willie Mays) to the laughter of his classmates. (Poor Charlie Brown, had the word been "mantle" as in one layer of the earth, it would have been spelled the same way as the other great New York centerfielder of the 1950s and 1960s, Mickey Mantle.)

In the cartoons, Charlie Brown was, of course, a loveable loser. He was often sad. He contemplated much of the negative side of life. Charlie's kite always got caught in a tree. His friend Lucy always pulled the football away from him as he ran up to kick it. And in baseball, Charlie Brown's teams always lost.

That is, until a wonderful day, March 30, 1993. On that day Charles Schulz created what is absolutely my favorite *Peanuts* strip of all time. While most of the *Peanuts* strips were three or four panels, this one consisted of a single panel that showed, like a stop-action camera might capture, Charlie Brown doing a cartwheel and other theatrics as he exclaims, "I hit a homerun in the 9th inning and we won! I was the hero!!"

Even more surprisingly, on June 30, 1993, Charlie Brown hit another homerun. (That homerun took a few days, and numerous panels to resolve as Charlie Brown rounded each base and slid into home on this inside-the-park game winner.)

Even Charlie Brown could be a hero. And if Charlie Brown could do it, so can we all.

Many of the issues facing those *Peanuts* children are the same issues facing us, and society, and schools in general, today. I'm not (yet) an expert on *Peanuts*, but I know for certain that as early as April 22, 1964, Linus was getting frustrated over the "new" math. Even today I hear parents, and some grandparents decry the "new math" of today. Little do they remember that the math they were taught was also considered "new" math.

Schools continually change and they continually look for new ways to solve old problems.

This type of change happens in other areas, not just schools. For many years I served on the Administrative Council of our church. I mostly enjoyed being on the committee. As the church transitioned through a number of head pastors, the vision of the church also changed, as did certain philosophies. I saw some old approaches removed only to come back again years later.

IMPOSSIBLE IS AN ILLUSION

My friends in business tell me of similar instances in their professions. What's old is new again. Yesterday's cutting edge approach is tomorrow's new paradigm.

In short, the old adage is often true - the more things change, the more they stay the same. I think the reason for this, at least in its purest form, is that leaders and workers who care always want to do better. I believe it is part of human nature to seek the very best solutions to challenges and problems.

Still, one negative aspect of this continual change is that, in our efforts to continually update our approach, we don't give enough time for what we are doing to take root, flower, and bloom. As a society if we don't see immediate rewards, we often seek quick changes and develop new approaches. Change is never easy. Change for change's sake often doesn't work and just as often leads to frustration, angst, and uncertainty. This is something leaders sometimes forget.

Sometimes, the old way actually works – quite well. Some old methods for selling probably still work today. Some standard medical practices that are effective remain unchanged for decades. And there are instructional approaches that teachers employ that are still effective in delivering material to students.

The key is for the leaders of an organization to trust the people who work for them. This is how one builds, creates, and maintains an effective organization. Great businesses are built on trust. It is the same for any successful organization including schools. There are many times when the workers, not the management, know the best ways to solve problems or get results.

While we need to continually grow, we should not automatically decry or discard techniques, methods, and approaches that work.

Sometimes the most cutting edge approach is leaving well enough alone.

And sometimes we just have to give things time. Great results don't always come immediately. Sometimes we just have to persevere. If given the opportunity to shine, people will always find ways to be successful.

Just like Charlie Brown. Even he hit a homerun.

Go team!

I Am Marshall

DR. PAUL SEMENDINGER

On Sunday, November 2, 2008, I had a most wonderful experience. Since I did not have the privilege of running the New York City Marathon that year, I decided to volunteer with The New York Road Runners and assist with the big race. They assigned me as a marshall in the post-finish area in New York's glorious Central Park. My assignment was to assist with crowd control as 39,000+ runners converged at the finish area. I was to keep the runners walking (and on the paths inside the park), help those who needed medical assistance ("MEDIC!"), and encourage the exhausted runners who had to walk the miles and miles through the finish area.

It was an inspirational and amazing experience. Within a few hours, tens of thousands of runners swarmed across the finish line, all converging on the same street in various forms of exhaustion. It was the marshals who asked the tired athletes to continue their treks down to the water, chip removal, package pick-up, and family reunion areas. When one finishes running 26.2 miles, he or she doesn't necessarily want to continue moving forward. It was our job to keep them doing just that.

Yet, in spite of the congestion, there was elation. There was passion. There was pride. There was accomplishment. The finishers obviously knew they were in and among thousands of others, but in a way they were also alone. Each and every one of the 39,000 finishers was alone. It was an interesting dynamic – one I'd never experienced from this perspective before. Each runner had come to a place – very personal and individual – as they accomplished a magnificent test of endurance and will.

They also shared their joy.

That day I received so many hugs, high fives, and warm smiles. Thousands patted me on the shoulders. For many runners, I was the first person to whom they were able to express their joy and pride.

IMPOSSIBLE IS AN ILLUSION

And when they saw me – sometimes in spite of a language barrier – they couldn't help but share their elation. One man just showed me his watch, smiling. Others expressed amazement at the caring nature of New York City and the job the volunteers did along the course. (One of the special aspects of the NYC Marathon are the thousands of volunteers and the millions of spectators.) Some finishers asked for medical attention – for them it was a hand around the shoulder and a walk to the medical tent. Others simply wanted direction – "Where do they take the chip from my shoe?" "Where is the water?"

But mostly, they were thankful.

Smiles and smiles and smiles. It was great to be a part of it.

To many people I was someone with whom they could share their happiness and accomplishment. I was a supporter. I was a special person with whom they could first share their excitement, exhilaration, and euphoria. And it was all glory, laud, and honor.

Yet, there were a few – not many by any measure, but a few, to whom I was not inspiring, but instead, saw me as a roadblock. I was the person who would prolong their pain. I was a rule maker or the enforcer who had no sympathy. "Just keep moving." I was the antithesis of kindness.

Central Park, like any park, has many exits. The first possible exit after the finish (and the medals and "heat" blankets) is at 69th Street. Finishers are not permitted to exit the park there. I was one of the marshals standing at, and blocking, the 69th Street exit. No one was allowed to leave at 69th Street. No one, that is, except VIPs, NY fire fighters, and the NYPD.

So in addition to congratulating the finishers, showing support, and being friendly, we had to remind the runners to "Stay to your right," and that "This is not an exit." That was fine and good, except when a fire fighter or police officer exited. Other runners didn't understand. "Police only, sorry," I'd say. Some finishers pushed past me. (They were soon met by police who made the point understood in a manner in which I was unable.) Some finishers begged, "I live right here." I understood, but I couldn't let them out.

Runners were instructed to keep walking (lest they create a log jam). I heard every reason: "Please, my friend is coming." "I just need a minute." "My wife is meeting me right here." To these people, I wasn't a welcoming sight. I had to ask them to keep moving. To them, I was a barrier and an inconvenience. I was someone who prolonged their pain.

It's a harrowing experience to run 26.2 miles and then be forced to walk at least another mile on aching, trembling legs. The runner has finished, he or she is elated. The dream has been realized. There is nothing quite like finishing a marathon. At that point many runners want to bask in the glory and elation. They want to rest. The marshals don't allow that. I didn't allow that. "Keep walking. Keep moving," I'd say. (I was, at least, very nice about it.)

This dichotomy made me think, a lot. At the same place, often at exactly the same moment, I was different things for different people. I was an instrument of good and the same time an instrument of frustration. It all depended on a runner's perception of what was right or fair, what they needed at the moment, and how they felt physically and emotionally.

The rules at the finish were established to create order and to help and protect the runners. With so many thousands of finishers, the race organizers know that room has to continually be made for the next person to finish. If we allowed the people in our area to linger, within moments there would have been a dangerously large human traffic jam.

IMPOSSIBLE IS AN ILLUSION

In addition, physiologically, runners should walk after running 26.2 miles. If a person stops too suddenly, he can cramp up or experience varied physical problems. Often a runner's rate of recovery in the days after a marathon depends entirely on what the runner immediately after completing the race.

But sometimes rules come when we don't want them. Some runners just wanted out. They were finished, physically and emotionally. These people couldn't bear the thought of walking further and further away. Yet that is exactly what we forced them to do. In a race as large as New York's, the ordeal after finishing often takes a marathon effort to get through.

Most of the runners understood. Most knew that we were all just volunteers giving our time to make the end of this experience as safe as possible for everyone.

I know that I wore a smile the entire time I was there. I was proud of what I was doing and honored to be giving back to a race that has always meant so much to me.

I think, in a way, my smile, my understanding pats on shoulders, and even the hugs let the runners know that I was there for them. I was an enforcer of rules, but I did this lovingly and respectfully. I know the emotions of finishing such an ordeal. I behaved as I hoped other marshals would treat me when our roles were reversed.

So often in life, a smile can make all the difference. A smile lets other people know that you care. A smile is a way to humble yourself before others. A smile welcomes people and opens up pathways to understanding and empathy.

At times some people equate a smile with weakness. They think if a person is happy, he can't be strong. Nothing could be further from the truth. In fact, if an individual is able to humble himself, that, by definition, indicates that he is strong. Only a powerful person can humble himself.

This smiling man enforced all the rules at the finish. It would have been easier to wear a frown and be a "tough" enforcer, but what would have been the purpose of that? Rather than being a beacon of joy to the finishers, I would have helped to make their finish experience even rougher. People would have avoided me. They would have steered away.

And, in the end, I would have lost out. I wouldn't have been given thanks. No one would have approached me with their smiles and hugs and unbridled joy. I would have had a long, tiring, and exhausting experience. What good would that have been?

Instead my smiles, and the runners' smiles, and our smiles together, added a positive exclamation mark to a most wonderful day.

Getting Better

DR. PAUL SEMENDINGER

*T*he following is a true story about how when a person strives to be the best, he brings himself, and others, to heights previously unimagined.

Our story begins with the most successful band in the history of rock and roll, the Beatles. The year was 1965. The Beatles were sitting on top of the musical world. In the previous three years they had charted no fewer than forty songs. Twenty-four of those songs reached the Top 40 and eleven became number-one hits. In that short time, the Beatles released no fewer than six albums that also reached number one on the charts.

The Beatles "yeah, yeah, yeah" style and sound was a defining aspect of popular music, but all of that was about to change...

As 1965 was closing, the Beatles released an album titled *Rubber Soul* that was, in many ways, a departure from the musical model that had brought them their unparalleled success. *Rubber Soul* marked the end of the Beatles existence as a strictly pop band and ushered in a new era in their history. The songs on this album were more complex and intricate and their lyrics were more thought-provoking. Even more than this, the sounds they made were unlike anything they had recorded before. History speaks to the significant change that this album brought to the Beatles:

"(Rubber Soul is) arguably the most important artistic leap in the Beatles' career– the signpost that signaled a shift away from Beatlemania and the heavy demands of teen pop, toward more introspective, adult subject matter. It's also the record that started them on their path toward the valuation of creating studio records over live performance. If nothing else, it's the record on which their desire for artistic rather than commercial ambition took center stage– a radical idea at a time when the success of popular music

IMPOSSIBLE IS AN ILLUSION

was measured in sales and quantity rather than quality." (pitchfork.com)

But as great as the Beatles were, *Rubber Soul* didn't just happen. The Beatles didn't just wake up one day and decide to invent a new way to record pop music. Rather, they were influenced by others, including a folk singer named Bob Dylan. Dylan's *Highway 61 Revisited* has been called the music that started the 1960s. In fact, according to *Rolling Stone* magazine, "Bob Dylan's influence suffuses Rubber Soul, accounting for the tart emotional tone of (many of the tracks)."

As true artists, the Beatles were not content to simply continue playing the chart topping pop music that brought them unmatched fame. As musicians, they listened to other artists and searched for ways to expand their own repertoires. The Beatles were not just a bunch of guys playing good music, they were innovators. They worked to understand each part and layer of a song's sound. They listened, they copied, they invented, and they modified. The result, *Rubber Soul*, was an artistic masterpiece that was unlike anything anyone had previously imagined.

Let's think about this in the context of professional development. There was no compelling reason, other than their desire to continue to explore music and their own talents and creativity that forced the Beatles down this road.

Put more bluntly, the Beatles had no reason to change. Changing would be messing with a formula that brought them unmatched success. The Beatles were already the top band of the era. In August of that very year, 1965, they were the first rock band to hold a major stadium concert. That year they performed for over 55,000 screaming fans at New York's Shea Stadium. They also starred in two hit movies. The Beatles were the gold standard in pop music.

Change wasn't just dangerous; it could have ruined their careers. But the Beatles weren't content with just being the way they were. They wanted more.

And it was this change that propelled them from being a good band to being considered one of the greatest musical artists of any generation. Yes, the music of the Beatles has been compared favorably to that of Beethoven, Mozart, and Bach.

Let's contrast what the Beatles did with what we hear from others across professions including education. Often times we hear people saying, "What I am doing is successful. There isn't any reason to change my approach." We also hear the old adage, "If it ain't broke, don't fix it."

Risks, especially creative risks, don't always work. Innovation is hard. Change is frightening. But when we change for the right reasons, because we know there is a better approach or a better way, then change can be transformative. That type of change can be awakening. Change for the right reasons can be inspiring.

When we change an approach because we want to be even better teachers for our kids, we are doing some of the most necessary work that can take place in a school building.

It has been said that good is the enemy of great. Society doesn't have great schools because it has good schools. Once organizations are considered "good," they often stop trying to get better.

We know that we can't stop improving when we get to good. We have to continually push ourselves forward. But even great isn't always enough. The Beatles were already great. They wanted to get greater.

IMPOSSIBLE IS AN ILLUSION

Rubber Soul became the first in a series of ground-breaking albums. The Beatles music and their approach was changing. But that's only one part of the story. The other part is how great thinkers and great doers are influenced by others and how that helps them become even better.

The other part of this story demonstrates that when we are challenged, and when we strive to be the best, we can reach heights that we never thought were attainable.

Just as Bob Dylan's sound inspired the Beatles, upon hearing *Rubber Soul*, another artist began to do some of the same self-reflection. That artist was Brian Wilson of the Beach Boys.

The Beach Boys were considered the Beatles' biggest rivals. From 1962 to 1966, twenty-two of the Beach Boys' singles cracked the Top 40. Like the Beatles, the Beach Boys were a hit-making machine. But when Brian Wilson listened to *Rubber Soul* he realized that the music in that album was well beyond anything that his band had ever considered, let alone, played. Spurred on by the Beatles' artistry, Wilson challenged himself to achieve a higher level. And so, while the rest of the Beach Boys toured the country, Wilson stayed behind in the studio writing some ground breaking tracks of his own. It was said that when the rest of the band heard these songs, the beautiful music moved them to tears.

Using Brian Wilson's new songs, the Beach Boys began recording their newest album, and the results were more impressive than any could have imagined. Inspired by *Rubber Soul*, the Beach Boys created an album known as *Pet Sounds*.

Just as the Beatles had done, the Beach Boys refined their sound and approach to music making. No longer were the Beach Boys just singing about girls and the surf and sun. They were embarking on a transition of their own.

Pet Sounds became the Beach Boys' most critically-acclaimed album. It is their masterpiece.

When we strive for success, when greatness becomes our singular purpose, the achievements we can attain are beyond imagination. When we allow ourselves to be immersed in striving for excellence, we can bring out abilities, talents, and skills that we never knew we had.

What is beautiful about this story is that the ideas from these creative geniuses pushed highly successful artists to even greater heights. Schools can do this. So can teachers. When we see teachers using innovative approaches to push learning and student engagement forward, we can be inspired to reflect on our own practices and to grow ourselves. That won't just make us better…that will make every teacher better.

Through healthy competition and a positive spirit, we can become more successful than we ever thought possible. Competition forces us to become even better versions of ourselves.

The amazing part about this story is that it doesn't end with the Beach Boys' signature album.

Upon hearing *Pet Sounds*, Paul McCartney of the Beatles was awed. He felt that the Beach Boys had produced something of a higher quality than anything his own band had ever produced. McCartney felt that the Beatles had been bested.

And being second best just wasn't good enough. So the Beatles returned to the recording studio with their most ambitious project yet…

IMPOSSIBLE IS AN ILLUSION

* * * *

Today, *Rolling Stone Magazine* ranks all of the albums I've mentioned in this essay among the greatest ever.

Here are the top five albums of all-time according to *Rolling Stone*:

5. The Beatles, *Rubber Soul*

4. Bob Dylan, *Highway 61 Revisited*

3. The Beatles, *Revolver* (This album was the Beatles critically acclaimed follow-up to *Rubber Soul*. It is apparent that they were hitting a creative peak. The recording of this album was in its final stages when Paul McCartney first heard *Pet Sounds*.)

2. The Beach Boys, *Pet Sounds*. (Time has proven Paul McCartney's initial feelings correct. The Beach Boys' most critically acclaimed album topped anything the Beatles had done to that point.)

But the number one album of all time, a musical masterpiece in its own right, cannot be left out of this discussion. You see, it was the influence of *Pet Sounds* that led the Beatles to record the number one album of all-time:

1.   The Beatles, *Sgt. Pepper's Lonely Hearts Club Band*

The Power of the Individual

◆

DR. PAUL SEMENDINGER

Sometimes when we hear about the achievements of people or groups that are highly successful we think, "That's great, but that can't be me." We often tend to downplay our own impact on others. We doubt our abilities to make a positive difference.

And, bluntly, sometimes that is easier. It is much easier to say, "I can't" than to go out and try to change the world, or if not the world, something in your own life. Often times, we look at the roadblocks, real or perceived, that will prevent us from working towards a worthy goal.

In the previous essay, I examined how the creative competition between the Beach Boys and the Beatles led them to create some of the greatest rock-and-roll albums of all-time. I think it's fair to say that if the Beatles hadn't recorded *Rubber Soul* then the Beach Boys would never have recorded their masterpiece album, *Pet Sounds*. It's also fair to say that without *Pet Sounds,* there would have never been a *Sgt. Pepper's Lonely Heart Club Band*. Each of these albums grew out of each band's desire to be the very best. Each band provided the creative energy and the creative competition to try to "one better" their rival. Each creative step forward pushed the bands to reach heights previously unimagined. It's an inspiring story.

This creative competition helped create legendary ground-breaking albums. The Beatles made the Beach Boys a better band, and the Beach Boys reciprocated in turn. The significance of this cannot be over stated. When we truly invest in our practice, when we truly desire to be the best, we become better than we ever thought possible. And our success, in turn, helps make other people better.

But, there is more to the story…

What we need to examine is the individual impact of just two musicians, Brian Wilson of the Beach Boys and Paul McCartney of the Beatles. Without those two individuals, the story of those albums and that creative genius never takes place.

Without Brian Wilson, there is no *Pet Sounds*.

Without Paul McCartney, there is no *Sgt. Pepper*.

You see, as the story goes, it was not the Beach Boys as a band that listened to *Rubber Soul* and were inspired to create something even better, it was Brian Wilson. Brian Wilson was the creative force behind *Pet Sounds*. That album was his vision – a vision he shared with his band. It was because of his passion, that the other members of the group were inspired to challenge themselves.

One could argue that *Pet Sounds* is really Brian Wilson's masterpiece that the Beach Boys just recorded and performed.

Similarly, there is no recorded history that George Harrison, Ringo Starr, or John Lennon of the Beatles were especially moved after hearing *Pet Sounds*; rather, it was the other member of that legendary band, Paul McCartney, who first set out to create something new and even more groundbreaking.

It was Brian Wilson and Paul McCartney, as individuals, who created the force and the motivation to set out and achieve even higher levels of greatness.

They had the vision. They took the risks. They inspired their colleagues.

That is the power of the individual.

All it takes to make a positive change in any organization, and in any situation, is one person. One person with the courage to say, "let's be better" or "I have an idea," can spark the next great exciting process.

One person can be the catalyst that ignites a staff or an entire organization.

The lesson here, and it's a powerful one, is that individuals can and do make a difference. The history of rock-and-roll, and modern music in general, was influenced not just by certain bands but by singular individuals in those bands who used their dreams and visions to push others forward.

This story forces us all to ask a central question of ourselves. We must ask, "What am I doing to bring myself forward?"

Next we each must ask, "What am I doing to help bring others forward?"

Your enthusiasm for a project, your ideas, and your positivity – simple as they may seem - can make the difference. You might be the spark that propels your business forward in ways no one ever thought possible.

It's a powerful thought to consider…

It all begins with you.

The Mystery Tour

We have spent some time discussing the competition and creativity that led to the success of some of the greatest rock albums of all time: *Pet Sounds, Rubber Soul,* and *Sgt. Pepper.* We have seen that creative rivalry can pave the way for greatness. We have seen that when pushed or inspired, people can achieve heights previously unimagined. We have also seen that it doesn't take large groups of people to start a new movement; it can really begin with just a single individual. To conclude this series, we need to talk about one other critical element of success – failure.

Following the success of the ground breaking *Sgt. Pepper's Lonely Heart Club Band*, the Beatles pushed the envelope even further. They decided to make a motion picture for television that documented a crazy bus trip across England. For this trip, the Beatles recruited a collection of unique individuals and filmed the exploits of this singular excursion. Of course, they also recorded music to go along with this "documentary" film. They called it all the *Magical Mystery Tour*.

While the musical numbers in this production were excellent, the final results of film and music together was, to be kind, uninspiring. The film itself was a disaster. Ultimateclassicrock.com describes the film as follows:

"The movie is a mess – incoherent, unfunny and an example of ego and authority running rampant and unchecked. *Magical Mystery Tour* proved that the Beatles were fallible after all."

The Beatles were fallible after all.

Halfway across the world in America, the Beach Boys ran aground in their own problems. Immediately following *Pet Sounds*, the Beach Boys recorded their greatest and most original hit "Good Vibrations." But following this single, the group faced their own disaster of a project. They gathered together to produce an ambitious album that would be titled *Smile*. It wasn't to be.

The *Smile* recording sessions were riddled with strife, angst, drug abuse, and other failings. The ideas and music that were supposed to be part of an album that could have catapulted the Beach Boys to their highest level yet, never came together. The album as envisioned was never released. The personal struggles of Brian Wilson, including depression, impacted his ability to write great music and be a contributing member of the band. Suddenly, the greatest days of the Beach Boys were behind them.

Two giants of popular music, coming off some of their greatest successes, had reached too far.

What can we learn from this?

First, the groups were not afraid to fail. Possibly by this time both bands felt that they could do no wrong. They may have thought that everything they touched would turn to gold. But I think it was more than that. In order to make it in the music business, individuals and groups face many failures. Even the Beatles famously failed to be signed after their first recording session audition. These artists knew that the opportunity for failure was always present. They did not, though, allow this possibility to inhibit their creativity. They took risks knowing that they might fail. (And in these endeavors, they did fail, at least to a point.)

Second, they did not let the failures define them. When they didn't achieve the accolades or successes they dreamed or hoped would come from the *Magical Mystery Tour* or *Smile* albums, the bands did not decide that they were now failures. Rather, they looked at their achievements, assessed where they reached too far, and continued following their passions – writing and recording music.

It is at this point that these two famous rock bands took different paths. As noted above, while they still recorded, the Beach Boys never again achieved the highest levels of success. They continued to produce and release records and singles. Some of their songs received modest praise and hit the charts, but none brought them all the way back to the top. The Beatles, however, still had a collection of chart-topping songs on the horizon.

Because they kept moving forward, these bands did not let failure become a permanent state. Failure is never permanent, unless we let it become permanent. One of the most damaging phrases in the English language is "I quit." When one understands the ebb and flow of success, one knows that failures are part of the process. Within each failure is the opportunity to learn and to grow. We don't truly fail until we stop trying.

Finally, it is important to realize that, within failure, there can still be positives. This aspect was especially true of The Beatles. Some of the most loved and original tracks the Beatles ever recorded are contained within the *Magical Mystery Tour* album. These include "The Fool on the Hill;" "Hello, Goodbye;" "I Am the Walrus;" "All You Need is Love;" and "Strawberry Fields Forever." Some of our greatest accomplishments can be parts of failures or set-backs. Within each failure is a learning experience. That is an important lesson to remember.

As we look within ourselves, we must have the drive, commitment, and willingness to seek creative solutions, to try innovative approaches, to be the individual person who makes a difference. As we stumble on our way to achieving our successes, we have to rise again knowing that the set-backs are just part of the process.

(As we get there, we might make great music, and we might even have a hit or two, but, ultimately, it is the journey that makes us all better.)

Why Not?

◆

Someday I will share the process I went through when I was selecting a college for myself. For now it'll suffice to say that the time it takes for my family to drive to visit and tour any one college with my son Ryan is vastly more time than I put into the entire process when I was preparing for this important life decision.

(That being said, I had a great college experience, and I credit King's College in Wilkes-Barre, Pennsylvania for providing me with an outstanding education that paved the way for a successful and very happy life.)

In our quest to find the perfect college for our son Ryan, we eventually visited Lafayette College in Easton, Pennsylvania. Lafayette immediately became Ryan's number one choice. It immediately became my number one choice and hope for Ryan as well. My wife Laurie feels the same way. We met Lafayette College and were immediately in love.

Lafayette seems like an amazing college. We have visited many great schools – any one of which we would be proud to send our son to, but Lafayette is just a little different. The standards are very high, and it seems prestigious, but at the same time, it felt…like home. We spent only a few hours on the campus, but it was a place I knew, immediately, where my son would thrive.

(TRIVIA – Lafayette College stands high on a hill in Easton, Pennsylvania. Easton is also the home of Crayola Crayons and the Crayola Factory. When our children were young, we toured and enjoyed the Crayola experience. (Is that a surprise?) Lafayette College is literally a stone's throw from the Crayola Factory, yet when we visited there, I did not even see the college or know it was there. There is a long future essay in all of this about what we take the time to notice, but, in short, sometimes, what we only see what we're looking for.)

IMPOSSIBLE IS AN ILLUSION

(TRIVIA II – Larry Holmes, the former boxing Heavyweight Champion of the World is from Easton, Pennsylvania.)

On to the main point...

Cur non (Why Not?) is the two-word motto of Lafayette College. It's a powerful and succinct message.

"Why not?" symbolizes the hopes and dreams that accompany each person as he or she ventures off to college. The entire college experience is, at its core, all about believing in the future and having the hope for eventual success. College isn't about now, it's about then.

"Why not?" comes from a statement made by the Marquis de Lafayette, a hero of the Revolutionary War, and the person for whom the college is named. Lafayette came to the colonies from France in defiance of French King Louis XVI's orders. Upon arriving in America, Lafayette sought out George Washington. They became immediate friends. In addition, Lafayette proved to be an able military leader who helped the colonists win the war.

Lafayette's feeling on whether or not he should initially come to America was summarized in the two words "Why not?" He had a dream – and he followed it.

I've always enjoyed reading and learning about Lafayette. He was a fascinating character. One summer, on what seemed to be the hottest day ever recorded, my family sat (patiently) with me in the blazing sun at Williamsburg, Virginia, just so we could listen to "Lafayette" (in truth, an actor, of course) give a speech to the visitors. This Lafayette was awesome. My kids still talk about how knowledgeable, interesting, and (yes) funny he was!

I'm not sure if the real Lafayette had a such a sense of humor.

DR. PAUL SEMENDINGER

Let's focus for a moment on the phrase, "Why Not?"

Lafayette's two-word slogan encourages individuals to look beyond what is probable and find out what is possible.

Why not? Take a chance, give it your best, anything is possible.

In the movies, Rocky Balboa utters a similar statement, albeit less articulately than Lafayette. When confronted by one of his biggest challenges, Rocky uttered, "Go for it."

If you have a dream – go for it. Why not?

You see, often when we strive to be great, we become great. No, not overnight. Along the way we face many struggles and failures. But when we set high goals for ourselves, and work to attain them, we find that we can succeed at tasks we never thought were possible.

I'd like to think that Lafayette would agree with me - impossible really is just an illusion.

I think, as educators, and models for youth, we need to consistently instill this spirit into the students we teach. Part of childhood should be about formulating dreams and hopes for the future. Every child has the potential to be great at something. Actually, many things. It is our responsibility as the adults in society, to build an environment that supports children until they are able to achieve their own goals.

We have to teach every child that anything is possible.

I am sometimes amazed when adults - teachers, coaches, clergy, neighbors, librarians, or shop clerks - look at children and see only who they are at that moment and not who they can be.
Every successful adult, of course, was once a child. In order for them to be successful, there were adults who believed in them.

IMPOSSIBLE IS AN ILLUSION

We must believe in children. We must believe in their futures.

Successful people also believe in themselves and work diligently to achieve their goals.

If you have a dream, go for it!

Cur non!

Two More Words

99% of the time I close my e-mail messages with the same two words. Some people might assume that I have this closing saved as my "signature." I don't. I write the same two words almost every single time I send an e-mail.

And there is a reason for this.

When I was in my doctoral program, I had the opportunity to spend time with one of the most respected former superintendents in New Jersey. This man mentored and guided all of the students in our program by offering his perspectives, thoughts, and ideas.

At the time, I was in my twenties, serving as the Vice Principal of Pompton Lakes High School, and my career was progressing at a fast pace. I knew that in a few years I'd have my doctorate, but I was smart enough to also know that I still had a lot to learn.

(If there is one thing I am good at, it is realizing that I don't know everything. I am amazed at what I don't know. I still have a lot to learn, and always will.)

In our conversations with this respected sage, the man whose reputation we all hoped to one day achieve, he offered practical advice on almost every aspect of leadership. He discussed making decisions, working as a team, and developing a vision. He also gave suggestions on simple things like how we should answer the phone.

I am glad I listened because he taught us that a few simple words can truly make a difference.

We were told that the best way to answer the phone is by stating our name followed by the simple words, "How can I help you?"

IMPOSSIBLE IS AN ILLUSION

The idea seemed crazy. As school administrators, we all knew that most times the people calling us weren't calling for idle chatter… they were calling because they were angry. Usually at *us*!

(I was a high school vice principal, remember. My job was to discipline kids. Every day. Fights, bullying, graffiti, cigarettes, drugs, runaways, truancy, failing… you name it, I dealt with it. If you asked little Ryan or Alex at the time what their Daddy does for a living, they'd say, "He suspends the kids." True story.)

While I respected this great educational leader, quite frankly, I thought his idea was unrealistic. Most professionals usually just stated their name, "Dr. Jones…" as their phone greeting. Nobody asked how they could help the caller. We weren't a store or a bank. People didn't call us for help; they called us to vent their concerns. Some called just to yell.

"This is Paul Semendinger, how can I help you?" – that's how our mentor suggested I answer the phone. REALLY?!

But you know what? Even though I wasn't convinced, I decided to try his approach. I went against my skepticism and started answering the phone in that manner. Soon it became a habit.

Darn if the old man wasn't right. Using those words made all the difference. People heard my words and were immediately put at ease. They felt less like fighting or arguing. Calmer discussions seemed to follow because I began each conversation by saying, "How can I help you?"

In addition to my words, the caller heard my unspoken message: "You might disagree with me, you might even be mad at me, but please know this… I do care about what you have to say."

I've been answering the phone in my professional life in that manner ever since.

* * * *

I hate to admit this, but, at that time (should I say, "In those days…"?) there wasn't a lot of e-mail.

I remember it was at about that time that *Kellogg's* first advertised having a web address. This was something I didn't understand at all. "Why do people need to go to a web site to learn about Corn Flakes?" I asked. "It's not like you can eat them on-line."

Back then, much of my professional interactions were on the phone. Today, not so much.

* * * *

Over the years, e-mail became the preferred method of communication. I started writing more e-mails. I also started receiving more and more e-mails.

Today e-mail correspondence makes up the bulk of my interactions with people – especially those outside of the staff and I often send or receive e-mails just to set up a phone conversation.

The world has changed.

And I'm not that old. I'm not. Really.

* * * *

For years, I'd close all my professional e-mails with one word – "Sincerely" – before signing my name.

IMPOSSIBLE IS AN ILLUSION

And then it dawned on me. Just like I answer the phone with a positive message, I ought to say a little more when I close my e-mails. "Sincerely" doesn't seem sincere. It sounds much too formal. I decided I needed a new closing.

I always liked the formality of the way people closed their letters in past centuries. As an example, in 1795, George Washington once closed a letter written to Thomas Jefferson in the following manner: *"With very great esteem & regard I am-Dear Sir Your obedt & Affectionate, Geo. Washington."*

Now THAT'S a closing!

But, all of that seems a tad bit too formal for today. So, while it's not all that original, I came up with "My Best," as my standard e-mail closing. I write this because when I say "goodbye" or "see you later," I want people to know that I really do send my best.

The words aren't just words... they are a true reflection of how I feel.

When I close an e-mail I am really saying, "I care about you, and I hope everything is good. I want to send you my best; my best for everything today and always..."

Doing this also keeps me focused on the fact that at the other end of the e-mail is a person who may or may not agree with what I am saying.

Some teachers might receive a "bad" e-mail (for example, "Your lesson plans haven't been submitted since February 1945") and think that I am mad at them. I'm not. I think the words "My Best" help to drive that point home.

A parent might receive an e-mail that recounts that their child misbehaved in school (for example, "Jimmy was seen throwing tomatoes at his teacher. To make matters worse, he missed with each of them.") and think I am angry with their child. I'm not.

I could save time by changing my e-mail settings and having "My Best," appear as my automatic closing. It would be easy because the words would appear automatically at the end of each e-mail I send.

That would be cool, but it would also be empty.

When I am writing an e-mail, I try to write in a way that is conversational. As I close, I send those words of affection hoping they are received and understood in the manner in which they are sent. This is because words matter.

Even two little words.

My Best.

Not Golf

DR. PAUL SEMENDINGER

*T*his story isn't about golf. Believe it or not, except for the miniature kind, I've never even played a game of golf - ever. But it's because of golf that I write this piece.

This is a piece is actually about the tremendous impact that we - as adults, as teachers, as members of the community - have on the lives of our children. How, as Haim Ginott once stated, "A teacher can be a tool of torture or an instrument of inspiration."

I'll begin by stating as I have so many times, that I have never been in a school, or any organization, that maintains such a positive and caring atmosphere as Hawes Elementary School in Ridgewood, New Jersey. The school is extremely special because the teachers have empathy and they are compassionate. The kids and their parents love the school because they know that the teachers and staff care, deeply, about their children. It's also why I love it there and why I am fortunate to be the principal.

So what does this have to do with golf? With patience, I'll get there. (Eventually.)

Interactions with other people can have a tremendous impact on the way we see ourselves. A smile from another person can cheer us up. A frown or a nasty word can do just the opposite.

They say smiles are contagious. I believe that.

But I believe frowns are as well.

* * * *

When my kids were young teenagers, we traveled to Universal Studios to see Harry Potter World. We loved it. Alex, our fifteen-

IMPOSSIBLE IS AN ILLUSION

year-old son was mesmerized. He was a devout Harry Potter fan. Alex was in his element!

In spite of the long lines, it was a great trip. The memories we created remain etched in my heart. In addition to the experiences on the rides and throughout the park, the gift shops were also special. Alex chose a magic wand and purchased his own Gryffindor robe. It was as if we were really at Hogwarts. (Today, Alex allows me to borrow that robe as I read *Harry Potter* to the fourth grade students at Hawes.)

But as nice as Universal Studios is, it isn't Disney World. As well designed, as well organized, and as enjoyable as Universal Studios is... it's not Disney World.

And I think I know why - smiles.

In Disney, there are more smiles. Smiles from kids, smiles from characters, smiles from adults. In Disney World, there are smiles in abundance. The people working at Universal were nice, but they weren't "Disney Nice." (I may have just invented a new phrase.) The workers at Universal didn't have the abundant cheerful demeanor that is found in the Disney parks. (That abundant cheerful demeanor is probably why I told my children many times that we should just live in Disney World.)

This difference impacts, in a subtle way, the entire atmosphere of the parks - from the moment you enter.

Disney seems to work hard, and succeed, in making everything wonderful (it *is* the "Wonderful World of Disney"). The building design, the atmosphere, the flowers - *everything* in Disney World seems to radiate with happiness.

The characters at Disney are happy - even the villains when you see them. Yes, even the supposed bad guys have smiles on their faces. Nice smiles, not evil smiles. Disney's focus though is on the happy characters - Mickey Mouse, Minnie Mouse, Winnie the Pooh, Goofy, and Pluto. Even the sadder popular characters, like Eeyore, are loveable.

Those Disney personalities are in direct contrast with the characters that Universal Studios showcases. Strolling around Universal they highlight Bart Simpson, Crusty the Clown, Thing 1 and Thing 2 from *The Cat in the Hat*, Sponge Bob, and others. Even at their nicest, these characters are edgy. They are often cranky, at times inappropriate and rude, and sometimes insulting.

That doesn't necessarily make them less funny, but it just makes the reaction to them a little different. They don't give me the timeless wonder of childhood that the Disney characters afford. Maybe I'm just more of a little kid at heart. (I never did want to grow up.) If I could choose with whom to play with, I'd pick Mickey Mouse over Bart Simpson. Every single time.

Universal is not Disney.

I saw this difference quite plainly as we were waiting on a long line to ride the mega-sized Harry Potter Hogwarts ride. The people on the (90 minute) line with us, as we looped and stood and looped and waited, were less happy (and some quite put out) than I typically see or remember from any long Disney line. There were fewer smiles. There was more angst and impatient postures from the "grown-ups." One guy continued to wear a backpack and disregard the frequent announcement, "You cannot bring backpacks on the ride; you must get a locker..."

I think, in a way, the Disney magic rubs off on the visitors each day. Sure, there are cranky people in Disney World and there are happy

IMPOSSIBLE IS AN ILLUSION

people at Universal. But there is a different feel to the two parks. In the same way, people comment that upon entering Hawes, there is a different feel - a more positive feel than at other schools. I agree. Hawes is a school that people immediately know is focused on kids and happiness, and joy and love. This isn't to say that other schools aren't great, just like I'm not saying Universal Studios isn't great. It is. It's just not Disney World. And other schools just aren't Hawes.

* * * *

But, I started off by mentioning golf. And I'll get there...

The reactions of others often have a tremendous impact upon us - especially the reactions of those we wish to please.

As a doctoral student at Seton Hall, we once had the opportunity to meet and hear from a renowned educational writer and speaker. This respected author came into our cohort to instruct us on her theories.

Being doctoral students in a cohort together, we all knew one another quite well. We took all our classes together and we had our breaks together. We ate together. We were together for three to four days a month, every month, for two years. I consider that a strength of the program.

One of the principals in our cohort was a strong (and very bright) woman from the Newark Public Schools where she served as a principal. We all respected her. Her comments in class always carried tremendous weight. Newark is a challenging place to be an educator. It's a tough city. New Jersey tough. And this school leader faced challenges that many of the other school leaders didn't ever face – or even have to contemplate.

At one point in the presentation, the famous author asked what we considered a successful day.

The Newark principal said, "A day without any problems."

The author, our guest, the renowned public speaker, author, and expert responded, "That's a shame." It was said with just the slightest bit of condescension or disapproval.

The principal who offered the comment took the remark as an insult (intended or not) and nearly broke down into tears. It was an amazing dynamic. Three words from the presenter changed the entire atmosphere of the room.

Such is the reaction when we feel that a person in power insults or belittles us – even if it is unintentional.

I often cite this interaction – If a grown successful woman can be insulted and made upset by a comment from a person in authority, who she doesn't even know, imagine the tremendous impact that we, as teachers, have on children.

This interaction is one I keep close to me as I know my reactions to students and staff alike can have tremendous weight. I want that impact to always be positive.

* * * *

And so we get, finally, to golf.

On our trip to Orlando and Universal Studios, I didn't have a lot of places to run. (I need to run.) As I was running on a path at the hotel "compound," I noticed a second paved path that ran parallel to the one upon which I was running. Since I was bored with the quarter

IMPOSSIBLE IS AN ILLUSION

mile loop I was stuck on, I ventured onto the new trail which happened to proceed around and through a golf course.

I ran over the hills and through the course and thoroughly enjoyed myself. This was a nice place to run!

A few days later, I went back.

This time, though, a rude guy pulled up next to me in a golf cart. He was a person of authority from the golf course. He began by saying, "No, no, no." I stopped and looked at him. He said, "You can't run here."

I replied, "Really?"

"This a private course," he said, unkindly.

"Oh, I didn't know."

"Where are you from?"

"I'm staying at the Hilton over there."

"Well, you better get off this golf course."

"Ok. Would you like to drive me out, or can I run out?"

"You can run out, but you must leave now." (The guy wasn't nice about any of this.)

"Ok, thanks."

And with that, I ran out of the golf course, as quickly as I could. (Yikes!)

What does this all have to do with Disney and Universal, and my old cohort member at Seton Hall, and Hawes, and perceptions?

Well (maybe I share too much of myself at times), that little interaction made me feel like, umm, (for a guy who tries to never curse, this is difficult)... I felt like... crud.

The man who scolded me, who was just doing his job (albeit with a bit of obnoxiousness), made me feel pretty darn badly. As Haim Ginott might have said, "He dehumanized me."

I felt a little better after I told my son Ryan about my escapade and he laughed at me. "Typical Dad," he said. That brought a smile to my face.

But, even today, years later, I feel badly about myself when I think of that interaction with the golf man. I wonder why I was so stupid as to think that I could jog around a golf course. Why didn't I know? When I have told this story to others, they have said, "Of course you can't jog there."

I'm not always the smartest of people. This small interaction reminded me how naive I can be sometimes. It still doesn't feel particularly good.

And I go to my main premise - if adults can be made to feel inferior or unworthy, or bad about themselves from others who don't even matter, imagine how kids feel when they hear or see the reactions from their teachers and the other important adults in their lives.

We have tremendous influence on children – even the ones who don't seem to listen to us. Sometimes those kids hear us more than the others. I am fortunate. I go to work every day in an amazing school. And every day I hear positive comments being made to children. Every day I see students arriving with smiles on their faces. Every day I see parents smiling as they drop off their children. Great schools can create a sort of magic. And it's wonderful. (Maybe we should call our school, The Wonderful World of Hawes.)

Just the other day I was with a teacher in a parent conference. "He loves you," the parent said to the teacher, referring to her fifth grader. That comment is typical.

Let's close with the acknowledgement that a theme park, or a business, or a golf course, or a school can definitely create a culture of happiness.

That culture of happiness is what can make the difference in the lives of others. Supportive and caring organizations have colleagues that respect and affirm each other. Great organizations have employees that affirm the clients. Most of all, the great places in society are the ones that lift up, value, respect, and love everyone – especially children.

Those are the places that are considered special. We can make them so. All it takes is kindness, affirmation, and love.

All of that… and a SMILE!

Mr. Miller

DR. PAUL SEMENDINGER

This essay is based on a story I have told countless times, but it's a story worth telling again.

I wrote this essay after receiving the news that the principal who first hired me as a teacher, Mr. David Miller, of Memorial Junior High School in Fair Lawn, passed away. Mr. Miller was 84. He lived a good life.

I was only fortunate enough to work for Mr. Miller for one year because he retired the year after hiring me, but it was a pleasure working for him. I have many great memories of my first year of teaching, but the following memory is my favorite and it was the most meaningful:

My first day as a classroom teacher had drawn to a close. I had met each of my five seventh or eighth grade social studies classes, and though I was a little nervous at first, I rose to the challenge. In fact, I thought I did well. The kids listened to me. They didn't act up. I was in control. It seemed like I could do this teaching thing.

To be honest, I was pretty excited to have successfully completed my first day as a teacher.

After the children left, I stayed behind in my classroom for a long while. I lined up the desks, washed the chalkboard, prepared for the next day, and completed a few other tasks. I didn't know quite how long I should stay at work. There was a lot I could have done, but I knew I was ready for the next day.

At some point I figured that I had done all I could so I got up and gathered up my things.

IMPOSSIBLE IS AN ILLUSION

On my way out of the building, I stopped by the main office to sign out. Mr. Miller was standing there. He said to me, "Paul, how was your first day?"

"Great!" I replied. "How was your day?"

Mr. Miller responded with words I can hear as clearly today as the moment he said them, "Paul," he said, "if your day was great, then so was mine."

The comment struck me. You see, I really believed Mr. Miller when he said those words to me. I thought that his day was great because mine was. I left the building after my first day of work feeling proud and successful. I was really glad I became a teacher.

Now, in retrospect, Mr. Miller may have been just saying any old response, but to me, those words meant something. I truly believed that Mr. Miller's happiness depended, at least in part, on my success.

And, as I look back, all these years later, I think those words were sincere because now that I sit in the same position Mr. Miller was in, I understand. My days are often contingent upon the successful work of the teachers at my school. Many of my best days are those when the teachers do exceptional things – or when they tell me about the exceptional things their colleagues or students have done.

This story, of course, shows the true impact of the words we say to others. People hear the words we say and remember them. Just like I remember, and treasure, the words Mr. Miller said to me… in September 1990.

September 1990 was a long time ago:

The President of the United States in 1990 was George Bush. The first George Bush. Since that time, we have had seven Presidential

Elections and four other presidents: Bill Clinton, George W. Bush, Barack Obama, and Donald Trump.

In 1990, the bombing of the World Trade Center was three years away. Yes, the first bombing...the one in 1993. September 11 was eleven years in the future.

Derek Jeter, the all-star baseball player, was still in high school, just starting his sophomore year. The Yankees, who people say "win every year" were a last place team in 1990. After a long and illustrious career, Derek Jeter, who played more games as a Yankee than any player in history, has now been retired for three years.

In 1990, Dr. Seuss was still alive. As were Miles Davis, Frank Capra, Redd Foxx, Fred MacMurray, and Danny Thomas (they all died in 1991). Leonard Bernstein and Aaron Copland were still alive. And so were Marlene Deitrich, Audrey Hepburn, Mary Martin...

Anyway, 1990 was A LONG TIME AGO.

In short, the words we say matter. They matter, especially, to children. What Mr. Miller said to me are words I will never forget. He validated me; he made me feel special. Mr. Miller made me feel important. With those simple words, Mr. Miller gave me the confidence to know that I mattered.

I was fortunate, many years later, to see Mr. Miller quite often when I coached two of his grandsons in baseball and soccer. I would always remind him of how much he meant to me. Sharing those happy thoughts were always good times.

Mr. Miller lived a great and wonderful life. In doing so, he touched my life in a positive manner. I will never forget his kindness and the great lessons he taught me.

June 11, 1995

*T*his is one of those stories that, at once, is hard to believe, but it is the absolute truth. This is one of those stories that remind us all that failure need not be permanent. This is true even for people who are considered the greatest of all time, for, you see, they weren't always considered as such.

This seems like a story about baseball, but more, it's a story about failure. And success.

Great success.

Great success that came only after dismal failure.

* * * *

On June 11, 1995, the New York Yankees, a fourth place team at the time, and not playing particularly well, faced the Seattle Mariners (a team that was playing pretty good baseball). They met at Yankee Stadium in the Bronx.

The starting shortstop for the Yankees that day was a twenty-year old kid named Derek Jeter. This would be just the thirteenth game in his budding Major League career. The great plays, the big hits, the World Series that would be coming were just dreams at the time. No one knew what lay ahead. At that particular moment, Derek Jeter wasn't anything spectacular as a big leaguer. On that day, he had an unimpressive .233 batting average with no home runs.

The starting pitcher for the Yankees was a scrawny twenty-five-year-old right hander named Mariano Rivera. Rivera was making the fourth start of his Major League career. To date, his performances had been even less remarkable than fellow rookie Jeter. In his

IMPOSSIBLE IS AN ILLUSION

previous games, Rivera had won once and lost twice. When he pitched, he gave up a lot of hits and a lot of runs. Eventually Mariano Rivera would become known for his coolness under pressure, but at the time people just wondered if this kid could pitch well enough to keep the Yankees in the game.

He couldn't.

The first batter for the Mariners hit a ground ball through the infield for a single. The second batter of the game hit a line drive to the outfield for another single. The third batter to face Rivera hit a home run into the left field seats. Before some fans had even found their seats, before others had mustarded up their hot dogs, the Yankees were losing 3-0.

Rivera eventually made it out of the first inning without any further damage and pitched just well enough in the second inning that no runs scored.

In the meantime, in the bottom of the second inning, Derek Jeter, batting at the bottom of the lineup, got his first at bat of the game. Jeter hit the ball all the way back to the pitcher for an out — certainly not the type of a result from which legends are made.

In the third inning, after getting an out on a long fly ball, Rivera allowed three of the next four batters to get hits. It wasn't pretty. Two more runs had scored and the manager was on his way to the mound to send Mariano Rivera to the showers.

His day was done. Mariano Rivera did not survive the third inning.

Remarkably, as a team the Yankees kept battling back. They started getting hits and scoring runs. Well, most of the players were getting hits and scoring runs. Not Derek Jeter.

In the fourth inning, Jeter grounded out.

In the fifth inning, Jeter struck out.

To be fair, it must be noted that in the waning moments of the game Derek Jeter did get a single and would later score a run in the eighth inning as part of a rally that would allow the Yankees to grab the lead.

In the coming years, the Yankees would win thousands of games in which Derek Jeter and Mariano Rivera took part. And in many of those games, Derek Jeter and Mariano Rivera were major contributors to the victories. But on this day, rather than winning *because* of Derek Jeter and Mariano Rivera, you might say that the Yankees won *in spite* of their performances.

After the game, the Yankees players had to pack their bags because the team was heading next to Detroit, Michigan, to play the Tigers.

Derek Jeter was particularly excited about this. Though he was born in New Jersey, Derek Jeter grew up in Kalamazoo, Michigan and for the first time in his life, he would be returning home as a bonafide Major Leaguer.

His bags were packed; he was ready to go…

But it wasn't to be.

Rather than traveling with the team to Detroit, Derek Jeter was told that he was being sent back to the Minor Leagues. Based on his performance, the Yankees decision-makers didn't feel he was ready to stay in the big leagues. But Jeter wouldn't be alone. Another player would be joining him - failed pitcher Mariano Rivera.

IMPOSSIBLE IS AN ILLUSION

On June 11, 1995, two of the most legendary players in Yankees history were sent to the Minor Leagues together. Their greatness, if it was to come, would have to come at another time. There was no guarantee that they'd ever be back.

In a very true sense, both Derek Jeter and Mariano Rivera had been given the opportunity to play Major League baseball and neither did well enough to stay in The Show. They both had to return to the minors to hone their skills, improve, and work their way back. For many players that trip back down to the minor leagues is the first step in the slow deterioration of their professional careers.

Most players don't ever make it back. They get sent down, the next great prospect captures someone's imagination, and a promising career slowly fades away.

It all happened so fast... and now it was over, seemingly before it ever started.

Derek Jeter and Mariano Rivera had failed.

* * * *

Success isn't always instant. Success isn't always guaranteed.

Even the greatest among us sometimes fail.

But the greatest, the ones who become winners, use failure as a motivation to work harder and try again.

Back in the minor leagues, Derek Jeter hit a solid .317 for the season. Away from the New York spotlight, forced to play in smaller cities and towns in front of fewer fans, Derek Jeter played liked the champion he would soon become. In September of that year, he returned to the Big Leagues.

The next season Derek Jeter was ready to fulfill his destiny. On Opening Day 1996, Jeter helped lead the Yankees to a victory over the Cleveland Indians. On that day he hit the first of his big league home runs. A legend was being born...

Mariano Rivera also kept working hard. He was back in the Major Leagues by early July. On Independence Day, Mariano Rivera pitched eight innings against the Chicago White Sox. In that game he allowed only two hits and struck out eleven batters. In September, the Yankees started using him as a relief pitcher. The position seemed to suit him. Soon Rivera was pitching brilliantly in the playoffs. The Yankees had stumbled upon a gem. The man who would one day save more games than any other pitcher - the man who would be considered the greatest relief pitcher of all time, had found his home.

The rest, as they say, is history.

To be the best, to achieve success in any endeavor, one must be ready to accept defeat. To become great, one must be ready to fail. To truly achieve, a person must know that he will stumble.

You only fail when you don't get up again.

You only fail when you give up trying.

You only fail when you stop trying to be your best.

Sometimes we think that greatness happens magically. It doesn't. Greatness takes guts. It takes perseverance. It takes learning how to pick yourself up when it seems you cannot go any further.

IMPOSSIBLE IS AN ILLUSION

Success comes when we work hard on days we'd rather just relax.

We achieve success when we are faced with failure and we resolve to learn from our mistakes and not let the failure define us.

At the start of their careers, two of the very best players in baseball history were sent to the minor leagues on the very same day. June 11, 1995 might be the single day that defined the spirit, the heart, and the character of the New York Yankees teams that would go on to win five World Championships Those teams were known for their grit, their character, and their perseverance even into the game's final at bats.

Maybe that was because the two greatest players on those great teams faced abject failure and were able to rise above that failure... to succeed far beyond anyone's imaginations.

Newton, Autographs, & The Teacher

◆

DR. PAUL SEMENDINGER

*D*uring his freshman year, Alex Semendinger sent me an e-mail from Williams College. In the message, he shared that he went to the Rare Books Library on campus and held a copy of *Philosophae Naturalis Principia Mathematica* written by Sir Isaac Newton. This is the text in which Newton came up with his laws of motion and gravity, the orbits of the planets, and so much more. The edition in Alex's hands was from the 1700s. Alex was amazed to be able to read and touch this famous work. It may have been an original copy. I imagine he was awe-struck.

I would have been.

In the early 1990s, my in-laws took my wife and me on a remarkable family trip to California. On that trip we saw many great and historical sites including Grauman's Chinese Theater. Grauman's is the place with all of the hand prints from the stars of Hollywood's Golden Age. My big thrill there was finding the Marx Brothers and putting my hand in the spot where Harpo's hand had been

Now, Harpo Marx was not quite the intellectual that Isaac Newton was (one could also argue that Isaac Newton wasn't half as funny as Harpo) but I can understand the thrill Alex experienced when he had the opportunity to "interact" with something, or someone, great.

The hobby of collecting autographs and memorabilia from famous entertainers and sports stars exploded decades ago to the point of over saturation. But before that happened, there was still something special about getting a relic or an autograph from a famous person. Actually, I think there still is.

There is something uniquely human about wanting to touch and interact with a historical artifact, a rare book, or a famous work of art. These are things that connect an ordinary person to someone or something great. The autograph provides tangible proof that, at least

IMPOSSIBLE IS AN ILLUSION

for that moment, a famous person was sharing time and space with you. This gives the ordinary person some connection with the famous. That autograph, in a sense, makes the ordinary person, somewhat less ordinary.

In fact, over the years, there are people who became (somewhat) famous just because they have gathered enormous collections of memorabilia. Barry Halper is one such example. Halper, for a time, had a collection of baseball relics, including autographs, that was said to rival the collection of historical items gathered in the Baseball Hall-of-Fame. Halper was famous, not for what he did, but for the size of the collection he gathered. There was the sense that he was more fortunate than others because his brushes with fame were more than most.

Today we see this same dynamic on the many shows about collectors or the stores they own. In fact, the store owners themselves are now seen by some as celebrities. All one needs to do is watch a few minutes of any episode of "pickers" or "sellers" to see people trying to connect with others who were more famous or who they feel are more important than they are.

The desire to connect with someone else – someone we consider more important than ourselves...

In the world of children, those important people are teachers; the grown-ups who make a difference. Teachers are the big people who bring joy, happiness, and love. They are the adults who share knowledge and the passion for learning with others. To children, these are the most important people.

If you don't think teachers are famous, think again. Just take an observer's view of a school on the day the students get their yearbooks. Who do they most want autographs from? Yes, the teachers. That says something.

Children actually want other "autographs," from teachers as well – not just those in a yearbook. These autographs might be the simple words that teachers leave on the tops of papers. Sometimes the "autograph" they want most is a sticker. Or a smiley face. Or a smile. All of these things are ways teachers affirm kids.

Words like, "great job" and "I am proud of you" (written or otherwise) are treasured in the hearts of children. These words affirm the work the child does, and like handprints, relics, or autographs, they bring the child closer to the person they admire – the teacher.

I sometimes sit in awe of the tremendous power a teacher has, the tremendous impact that a teacher can have on a child's self-image both now and in the future. Teachers can use their autograph, their imprint on a child, to change a life. These positive words bring children closer to the biggest heroes they will ever know. The positive words teachers leave can inspire children to work harder, to give more, and to be better.

Although a baseball from Babe Ruth will always be sold for more money, I honestly believe that the words, *"You did GREAT! I am VERY PROUD of you. Love – Your Teacher,"* will always be more valuable. Significantly more valuable.

Teachers should always look to make a positive difference on children by giving the gift of their autographs on their work and the gift of their smiles that comes from the love in their hearts.

To students, teachers are the biggest heroes of them all. Teachers are greater than, well, anyone. They are greater than Isaac Newton.

Teachers are even greater than Harpo Marx – and *that* says a lot!

Experts

DR. PAUL SEMENDINGER

*E*arly each school year I read a wonderful picture book titled *The OK Book* to a number of early elementary classes. The book, in short, tells the tale of a person who is not very good at things, but who keeps trying nonetheless. After finishing the book, I have a discussion with the students about always trying, even when we fail.

One time, our discussion focused on the idea of trying many activities and working hard to become good at one thing. I asked this group of second graders, "Is anyone here an expert at something?" I was anticipating no hands to be raised so I would then be able to say, "But, if you work hard at something, you can become an expert."

To my absolute shock, virtually every student raised a hand. I kept thinking, "Experts, really? They are seven years old! We're good, but we're not that good." Then I thought, "Wow, this is great, they such positive self images…"

I had to probe further. Maybe seven-year-olds are experts at things. I think kids are better than grownups at playing with toys, for instance. Kids are also much better with imagination. Kids have a limitless supply of hope. Children are definitely not cynical. There are many things we can learn from kids. I wondered if seven-year-olds were able to know this? (Can someone who is not cynical understand the cynical nature of adults?)

Some of the students proceeded to tell me the areas in which they were experts. It became very apparent that they were not thinking as I was.

The children told me they were experts at baseball and dancing and piano and gymnastics. Part of me wanted to correct them ("Well, you might be good, but are you an expert?") but I let it go.

IMPOSSIBLE IS AN ILLUSION

It was cute and fun and nice. Not all lessons are successful. I don't think the children got the main point of my discussion.

I moved on and thought about how to approach that lesson more effectively in the future, and then I didn't think much about seven-year-old experts for a few days.

Then, during a walkthrough of a kindergarten class, a teacher showed me, among other things, lists the children made of areas in which they considered themselves experts.

The kindergarten kids believed that they were experts in writing, cars, dinosaurs, pizza, girls (I did a second take on that one - it was a girl, thank goodness), school, reading, skiing, and many other areas.

The teacher explained to me that in the kindergarten curriculum an expert is defined as someone who knows four or five facts about a subject. I started to laugh. "If that's an expert," I said, "now I know why so many second grade kids told me they were experts… because by that definition, they are."

As I thought more about this, as cute as it is to see little children professing to be experts in certain things, I had to take pause. Words are powerful tools. When we use words incorrectly, we actually hinder the ways in which we communicate.

The curriculum that asks for teachers to call children experts because they know a certain number of facts, I think, does them a disservice. Is that really what an expert is? I know a lot about a lot of things, but I am certainly not an expert in any of them.

In fact, I believe that the more I learn, the more I realize that I have a lot more to learn – about everything. I worry about people thinking they are experts just because they know a few facts. That's probably the wrong lesson to teach kids.

I also think that we often devalue words in society. By trying to build up children by calling them experts, we are actually devaluing real experts – people who have worked their entire lives to become the among the best or most knowledgeable in their field.

The experts I know and have read about continually work at their area of expertise. They don't stop after acquiring a specific number of facts or skills. They don't halt their progress and state, "I am now an expert." No, they keep working. The most successful people always reach for more and strive for greater things. They do not rest on their laurels. In fact, when they back off, they often see themselves falling further and further behind.

A virtuoso on an instrument, for example, spends countless hours, daily, at his or her craft. This doesn't come easy. The person doesn't say, "I know five scales, I'm done." No, they continually thirst to improve their technique, their skills, and their understanding of music. That's what a true expert does.

How does that, at all, compare with a five-year-old that knows a certain number of facts about dinosaurs? While I love the idea of sending kids the message "You're great at so many things," using the word expert to do this is misguided.

We can say, "You know a lot about that." We can say, "You certainly worked hard." We can state that we're impressed with their knowledge, but we shouldn't devalue experts by calling little children experts (unless little Mozart is in a classroom) when the skills they demonstrate are far from that lofty level.

I also think this devalues the children themselves. It teaches them that they have attained the heights necessary and that they don't have to strive any longer. Why do we want to foster that spirit in children? We should instead instruct them on what it takes to become an expert and foster the motivation necessary to push students to achieve that level.

The other lesson I learned, though, is that the word "expert" had a different meaning for the students and for me. In spite of my protestations, the word is part of these children's vocabulary in a particular way. We used the same the word but meant entirely different things.

I wonder how often this happens in our communications with each other. I wonder how often we say the same thing, but our words are heard differently. I wonder how often we miscommunicate, even when we think we're being clear.

Have you ever been in a heated discussion with someone and realized you were both saying similar things, albeit differently and that you actually agreed rather than disagreed? It's happened to me.

Words are powerful things. One thing we should teach children is how to be precise with their word usage and how to use words properly.

The English language is very rich with great words that mean very specific things.

Something that is great is not necessarily magnificent. The words are different.

Something wonderful is not necessarily spectacular.

An angry person isn't necessarily mad.

The English language is fascinating and it is a wonderful tool for great communication provided we use it correctly.

Learning this would be a great way to invest our time in schools. In fact, if we can use our language correctly, we might be actually become reading and writing experts.

What Classical Music Can Teach About Quality Instruction

◆

I enjoy music. Most people do, of course. Depending on our mood or purpose for listening, we enjoy different music styles at different times. When I run, I usually like up-beat fast-paced music with motivational lyrics or I simply just listen to the songs from the Rocky movies. Other times, quieter music will suffice. A little Sinatra goes a long way when I complete some of my daily routines such as washing the dishes or straightening up.

I have also found that listening to classical music provides me with a certain peace and tranquility. The more I listen to classical music, the more I enjoy it. It is a growing infatuation.

For much of my life, I tried to enjoy classical music, but a few things got in the way.

The first was a sense that the classical music canon was too overwhelming. There was too much to learn and it seemed to encompass everything. I didn't know the difference between Mozart, Beethoven, and Bach. (On many levels, I still don't.) Besides the big names, there seemed to be thousands of other composers and artists who I never heard of. Figuring all of that out just seemed impossible.

Whenever I would try to listen to classical radio, I was always awed by the announcer who seemed to say something like, *"That was the Hummingbird Dance Suite in D-Minor by Luciano Flaboricchio, recorded by the Prague Philharmonic and conducted by Flaustvious Cordova with flute played by Nikkoli Ramdumson III."* In short, I could barely understand what the announcer said and knew no way of figuring it out. (Classic rock radio is much easier to understand - *"That was The Beatles with 'Day Tripper'."*)

The second stumbling block was the fact that I thought I had to actually understand classical music in order to enjoy it. I thought each song had a purpose and a message and that I had to figure it out. That is how classical music was taught to me when I was a child. I remember lessons in elementary school music class with the teacher saying things like, "*Now if you listen closely, you will hear the horses arriving on the battlefield...as they arrive the archers take their aim and maim the lead character, Odysseus. The song then transforms into a melancholy arrangement of sounds until doves arrive and carry the protagonist to the heavens.*" I will admit here that I thought I was stupid and that I was the only person who only heard instruments and noise. There may have been some nice sounds, but none of them sounded anything like horses, arrows, or birds. The piece would end and I'd still be waiting for the cavalry to arrive.

I also didn't know the sounds various instruments made, so I'd be lost when the teacher would say, "*Now listen for the French horn as it brings with it such supreme majesty...*"

My efforts to understand things that were beyond my comprehension ("*Notice the chord progression as the piece shifts into the minor key*") also blocked me from enjoying great music. If I had to understand it, I couldn't enjoy it.

It's much easier to listen to "*She loves you, yeah, yeah, yeah...*" Now that I can understand.

On top of this, the various classical eras confounded me, even into adulthood. What is the difference between a song from the Baroque period and a song from Renaissance period? Some Romantic songs seemed the opposite of what you'd expect for a quiet dinner with someone special. And, if it's all classical music, how can there be a Classical music period?

Who decided to make this all so difficult?

Then there is the length of the songs. *Rhapsody in Blue* runs for over seventeen minutes. Mozart's *Symphony No. 40* runs for at least thirty minutes. Of course, these are just two examples. Contrast that to "Hey Jude" by The Beatles which pushed all boundaries by running over seven minutes. And that was a long song. Billy Joel sings (in "The Entertainer"), *"If you're gonna have a hit, you gotta make it fit, so they cut it down to 3:05."*

Still, I always had a fascination with classical music. I wanted to like it. Over the years I have tried many different methods to kick-start a passion or at least an understanding of it – subscribing to classical music magazines, reading biographies of composers, listening to many "Top 100 Classics Of All Time" albums and CDs...and yes, even trying to play some easy classical pieces on the piano. (I can fake my way through parts of Beethoven's *Fur Elise* and the beginning of *The Moonlight Sonata*, but, trust me, you wouldn't want to listen.)

One day, I said to myself, "I'm not going to try to remember all these composers and artists and genres."

Instead, I decided, "I'm not going to try to understand it; I'm just going to try to enjoy it."

Now I mostly just listen. And I have found that I really do enjoy the music.

I share all of this for a few simple reasons:

First, I think my experiences with classical music touch upon something that we, as educators, often fail to think about. When children don't learn certain things, it may not be for a lack of trying or even interest. It might be because the presentation confuses them or makes the material non-accessible. EVERY early interaction I had with classical music made it inaccessible to me. I couldn't enjoy it

IMPOSSIBLE IS AN ILLUSION

because I always thought I had to find a secret meaning or understand complex music theories.

(Just for the record (no pun intended), I see this in many disciplines. This frequently happens in sports. I see it a lot, coaches shouting instructions such as, *"Don't just swing the bat, line-up your knuckles, keep your back shoulder even, stride with the front foot, recognize the pitch, turn your waist, wait, think about what you want to do with the bat when it hits the ball..."*

In my opinion, that does not help a kid learn to play baseball. Sometimes the best instruction is just *"Try to hit the ball kid."*)

When children aren't learning, sometimes the obstacle standing in their way is...us.

Second, we should always encourage all our students (and ourselves) to continually grow and try new things. Invite them to look for new skills and new ideas they enjoy. Too often we let people say, "I don't like ____." I think children (and all of us) are too young to write things off. We need to continually encourage our students to gain skills and appreciation for academic (and other) pursuits.

Third, we need to make sure that as educators we always bring a sense of fun and discovery to our lesson development. While we need to know that it is sometimes ourselves that erect barriers to learning. We also must always remember that it is our enthusiasm for learning that rubs off on the students. Students love school when their teachers love school.

I always am inspired when I see teachers who allow children to discover. I imagine that I would have enjoyed classical music more as a child if the teacher played small parts of songs and just asked us what we heard – and then valued our responses. If we didn't hear a humming bird, but instead envisioned a motorcycle, maybe the teacher should have asked why. She could have learned from us! That would have been empowering!

Fourth, we must always watch the length of our lessons. When we talk too much, we are like that inaccessible symphony. What kid can pay attention through all of that? Less teacher talk – more student engagement – that's a key. In order for students to learn, we have to let them learn. They learn by doing, not necessarily just by listening.

Finally, when we are excited about something, and we share that excitement, others become just as enthused. We have to share that excitement with the students. More, we have to share that enthusiasm with our colleagues – and even the administrators. We can learn and grow, continually, from one another. Kids learn from watching us learn.

In short, it is up to us, always, to make the material we teach accessible, interesting, and meaningful for students. We need to let kids engage with our lessons on their own level and in their own way.

When we do that, we are truly teaching! When we do that we're creating masterpieces.

When we do all the things necessary to create environments of learning, we are creating a symphony of wonder!

Bravo!

We Choose the Moon

"But why, some say, the moon? Why choose this as our goal? And they may well ask why climb the highest mountain? Why, 35 years ago, fly the Atlantic? Why does Rice play Texas?

"We choose to go to the moon. We choose to go to the moon in this decade and do the other things, not because they are easy, but because they are hard, because that goal will serve to organize and measure the best of our energies and skills, because that challenge is one that we are willing to accept, one we are unwilling to postpone, and one which we intend to win, and the others, too."

John F. Kennedy
September 12, 1962

I chose, as you see, to begin this passage in a different way, opening with a quote rather than my own words. These lines of inspiration are greater than I could ever write – and delivered more powerfully than I could ever deliver them. I wasn't alive when President John F. Kennedy stood before crowd of thousands at Rice University to tell the nation about his ambitious plans for the future, but I am energized and motivated every time I read or listen to his words.

I am inspired by the notion of doing something great, not because it is easy, but because it is hard. In a sense, it's how I have lived my life. I abhor the simple and push myself intellectually, physically, and in many other ways to rise above any challenge.

Because the wonderful school where I work has a dynamic and energetic space studies program, I have invested a great amount of

IMPOSSIBLE IS AN ILLUSION

time studying the history of space exploration and have learned a great deal.

In 1962, going to the moon, ever, let alone in fewer than eight years, was a goal that was lofty to say the least. Many thought it was impossible. In fact, by any logical standard - it *was* impossible.

And yet, they did it. (Impossible is, after all, an illusion.)

They did it for many reasons, not least of which was the fact that President Kennedy's words inspired many people to get the job done – to make his dream a reality. He set up a timeline, outlined the goals, and gave people the push. His words were the catalyst. Individuals by the thousands took those words to heart and did what they had to do to make the dream come true.

And they did it!

Of course, the careful reader knows what's on my mind and quickly surmises the overall premise of this passage: *"If they could go to the moon, then surely, anyone, anywhere, can, with enough hard work and determination, achieve any goal."* Alas! You're right. That is my focus.

Once we set a goal, we must work passionately to achieve it. We need to be creative, focused, and diligent on a daily basis. We must take every possible step to assure that our goal is achieved.

This is not to say that many people don't already do these things. Of course they do. President Kennedy wasn't saying that the United States had not done great things previously. In fact, in the longer speech he mentioned many of these accomplishments because he understood the struggles and the achievements that the Americans had made.

Yet, he pushed us to even greater heights.

You see, we cannot rest on our laurels. We cannot say that we were great... last year. We cannot even say that were great... yesterday. We need to be great today. And we need to be great tomorrow.

Even more than that, we need to be even greater tomorrow.

We must never stop striving to be better.

As Jim Collins in his powerful book *Good To Great* states: "Good is the enemy of great."

In short, we don't have great organizations, principally because we have good organizations. The fact that people or organizations are good often blocks their ability to become even better. Good becomes "good enough."

We can never say we are good enough. In fact, good enough never is.

A World Series Championship team doesn't head into the next season content to just play the games and possibly lose. No, they play to win again. The greatest teams in the history of sports are not one-time champions. The greatest teams are the teams that win again and again and again.

In order to do be continually successful, it takes hard work, diligence, and focus. It takes a willingness to push beyond initial success to find even greater success.

I am hoping to be a successful author. I hope that readers love this book and are inspired. I have invested untold hours writing, revising, and editing my words. And I'm never quite satisfied. Sometimes I get hung up on a single word. I gave up rest and sleep and ease to get

IMPOSSIBLE IS AN ILLUSION

this done. And I am glad I did. Still, I hope my next book, whatever that is, is even better.

If someday I write The Great American Novel, am hoping that the follow-up to that is even better.

I hope my best softball season is the one yet to come.

I hope my fastest marathon is the one I am currently training for.

I don't ever want to say, "I was better back then." No, I want to say, and really believe, that I'll be better in the days to come.

And yet, there is a little more to this story.

In the speech mentioned earlier, President Kennedy set a second goal – a huge goal – that often times does not get noticed. He said more than we just have to go to the moon successfully. He said, "…and the other (things) too."

The Other Things.

President Kennedy didn't define the "other things," probably because they can't be defined or maybe because there are too many "other things" to ever list. I believe it is these "other things" that define a person, and organization, a family, a business, or a school.

I believe it is the other things that make someone great.

We have great organizations because we have people who care enough to make them and keep them great. Programs are developed, invented, and improved upon. People in successful organizations don't look to achieve greatness once and in just one area – they strive to achieve and achieve some more.

Amazon was once just an on-line book store, but today a person can purchase almost anything from Amazon. And they didn't stop there. Amazon also looks for new ways to deliver the items you purchase cheaper and faster than through any other fulfillment service. There was never a time before Amazon, when a person could ever expect same-day delivery for something purchased over the internet. But we have that today because Amazon keeps looking to get better.

Amazon isn't satisfied with just being the best.

I love Disney World. I love the rides and the attractions and the joy that comes from always trying to be childlike. The rides at Disney World are amazing. Each time we visit, we try to experience as many rides as possible. I often leave feeling that I have experienced all that Disney has to offer. And then I find out that they have added new rides and created new experiences.

Disney is certainly not satisfied with just being the best.

That is the spirit and the character of a winner, of a champion, of an achiever, or a successful organization.

President Kennedy said they would achieve the main goal, bringing a man to the moon and returning him home safely, which they did – but he also added, *"and the other things too."*

That is what makes all the difference. As we strive to meet our biggest goals, let us keep in mind, and also continually focus on "the other things too."

The End

I'm sad as I write this, sincerely and truly sad. Empty. Reflective. Melancholy. Somewhat regretful. Definitely out of sorts.

I never thought I'd feel this way about this. It's one of those things that when the time came, I thought relief would be the overriding feeling.

I sincerely thought this would be one of those, "Well, I survived enough of them" moments.

We've all had those moments - times when we are glad a certain task or obligation is over. This feeling usually brings a sense of relief. "Whew, I'm glad I don't have to do *that* again."

Instead, now that it has come, I'm sad. I'm sadder than I ever thought I'd be about this.

* * * *

Tonight is one of those Long Principal Nights. I have a lot of these throughout the year. Nights like this keep me at work well into the night – sometimes, literally, past my regular bed time. These are nights of dinners alone as I attempt to get important work completed prior a meeting or an event. And, no, it's not always an opportunity for my favorite food, pizza; stretched for time, tonight I had a yogurt. (Leadership isn't always glamorous!)

In the course of my career, I've had countless nights like these. I think only my wife and kids truly know how many hours I work each week. In many ways, the little office where I write this is my second home. Please know, I'm not complaining. I love my job. I love investing in my school for the entire community – the teachers, the parents, and, of course, the children.

IMPOSSIBLE IS AN ILLUSION

It has been said that when you love your job that work isn't work. And, most often that is very true. I have invested the very fibers of my being into the schools where I have worked because of my pure love for everything about education: kids, teachers, families...and learning.

But it is because of tonight, and the fact that I have to work late, that I am a bit sad.

* * * *

You see, life goes too quickly. It flies. Sometimes we don't think it flies, but it does. Just when we think it's going slowly, life hits us square between the eyes.

For example, I find it hard to believe that I'm 48 years old. I remember when my dad turned 40 and we all thought that was old. Wasn't that yesterday? (My dad is now 78 years old. I don't think of my dad as an old man, but 78...yikes! Where did the time go?)

In a few weeks, my youngest child will be 18. Little Ethan Sem will be 18. How is that possible?

I have to wear reading glasses more and more to see stuff that is written down. How is *that* possible? Yesterday I was a young guy.

All of this is happening too quickly. Where did the time go?

* * * *

The older I become, the more I don't get upset about the little things in life that can be frustrating or upsetting. I think that's a good thing. I have learned that the little things pass. I address them. I deal with them. Sometimes they make me sad, or reflective. But I don't let the little things bother me as they used to. This might be what they call maturity.

I have also learned that the big things pass too. They really do. In the scheme of life, many of the big things we worry about aren't really big things. Think of the situations or conflicts that most upset you last year, or five years ago. Many of those things, I am sure, matter not at all today.

At the same time, I have also learned to try to savor the little things that are good. I was never like that before. Ever. I rushed through everything. I still do, most often. But now, sometimes, when I really think about it, I try to embrace little things more. I try to appreciate almost everything.

I'm not real good at this yet, but, I'm at least aware and I'm trying…

Sometimes, as parents, we have to do things we really don't want to do. I tried (and try) very hard to be a great dad. I think that's my most important job. I tried to "be there" and be involved with every aspect of my sons' lives as they grew up. I ran trips, I camped, I coached countless teams, we traveled, we played games, we watched movies, we read books, and we did a lot of fun stuff. It was great…but not everything was fun.

It's never all fun.

Sometimes I cared about things I shouldn't have. I may have even been unreasonable at times with messy rooms and toys that weren't put away. Now that my kids are grown, I often long to see cars, trains, dinosaurs, blocks, and marbles lying around. I miss those things.

I will admit here that sometimes I felt obligated, as a dad, to attend events or programs that I didn't really want to. For example:

IMPOSSIBLE IS AN ILLUSION

My kids were in some concerts that weren't very good.

It's no fun sitting (even if one is the coach) outside at a soccer game on a rainy, damp, and cold Sunday in November. (This is especially true if your team loses 8-1, which seemed to happen more than enough times to my teams.)

All of the Boy Scout campouts weren't necessarily fun. The kids that go along aren't necessarily all pleasant, kind, or respectful. (Imagine that!)

After my kids' elementary school years, I didn't really enjoy going to many Back-to-School Nights. Those became a bit of a drudgery.

But believe it or not, that's why I'm sad.

Tonight I have a work obligation that's taking me away from Ethan's final Back-to-School Night. Over the years, I've missed my share of events - it's part of the job I have. When I am at work, I can't be "there" – and the schedules for my kids' school events were always very similar to mine. But this was a little different. This was my last ever Back-to-School Night as a dad, and I missed it.

I'm sad because this was something I thought I'd be glad had passed. But now that it has, I wish it hadn't. I'm sad because when I left Back-to-School Night last year, I didn't realize that I'd never pass that way again.

I'm sad because it's over. And now that it is, I'd like one last crack at it.

* * * *

Life passes too quickly.

Our parents age too fast.

Our kids age too fast.

We age too fast.

And so, as a result, we have to embrace life while it happens. We have to savor the moments, all of them, even the ones we don't think we'll miss, because there will come a time when even those things will end. When that happens, we might be surprised when we miss those things.

We have to learn to cherish each day. There is so much good. It's important to notice it – to embrace it – and to love it.

I never thought I'd miss Back-to-School Night.

But I do.

Life is Easy

◆

DR. PAUL SEMENDINGER

I'm not a philosopher. (It would be tough to call anyone who often quotes Rocky Balboa a philosopher.) Still, I do try to share some - deep thoughts in my writing. As I have aged and collected a few decades worth of knowledge, I have been drawn to some great thinkers. For example, I have grown very fond of Ralph Waldo Emerson and I recently purchased one of his books (*Self-Reliance and Other Essays*) that I greatly look forward to reading.

Confucius is another great mind of history that I have been drawn to recently. His philosophies, written 2,600 years ago still resonate today. I figured that I'd take some time to examine just a few of the many statements left to us by Confucius to see how they relate to our lives as educators and teachers of children.

"Life is really simple but we insist on making it complicated."

We begin with a statement that shatters a lot of what we like to say about "the world today." Most people (I think really all of us) like to shake their heads and state that life today is hard – and that it's harder than ever. But Confucius was born in 551 BC, and people back then were also saying that life was hard. You know why? Because it was. Life was hard in 551 BC. It was hard in AD 135. Life was hard in 1276 and in 1842. Life was hard in 1935. I tend to think that life today is not harder than at any other time in history; we just don't know the other times – because we don't live in them. I don't think there was ever a period of time when people just sat around and said, "You know, life is really easy. I have no troubles and no worries."

Life today is just different. It's not harder. Yet, like people from every generation, we often do make it more complicated. You see, part of the human condition is to obsess over the struggles we go through rather than focusing on the good. When we obsess over our troubles, we end up making life more complicated.

IMPOSSIBLE IS AN ILLUSION

I think this is also true of teaching. We often make the task harder than it needs to be. Good teachers know how to connect with kids. Good teachers know what works. It is not difficult: have energy and passion, be engaging, develop great plans, smile, respect kids... When teaching becomes hard it's often because we are making it unnecessarily difficult.

There are times when teachers are provided with resources that are designed to make things easier – and there are times when these suggestions, guides, or best practices can be helpful. But sometimes, they just make the process more complicated. Some best practices aren't the best and really are just practices. Suggestions are great, and can be wonderful, but too much information, can be…too much.

Many years ago, the great Yogi Berra was in a batting slump. He listened to all the suggestions offered to him from all the experts on how to regain his hitting stroke. He tried a number of different approaches. None of them worked. Yogi finally commented, "I can't think and hit at the same time." The experts had complicated the formula. Once he stopped thinking, Yogi started hitting.

When we consider the challenges we face on a day-to-day basis, I would assume that many come from barriers that we erect ourselves. Most of life, most of the time, is simple: Work hard, be kind. Give. Laugh. Share. Love. Follow the golden rule. It is a simple formula. Sometimes we just need to get out of our own way.

"Everything has beauty, but not everyone sees it."

When we uncomplicate our lives, when we simplify, we often find that we have more time.

More time allows us to look closer at the world around us. When we look at the world with open and relaxed eyes, we can see beautiful things that we never noticed before.

Confucius was right. Given enough time, we can find beauty almost everywhere. But it's not just every*thing* that has beauty, as teachers we must also remember that every person has beauty, but not everyone sees it.

To start, we often don't see the beauty in ourselves. When we are caught up in making life complicated, we often fail to recognize and appreciate all of the things we do to make the world a better place for ourselves and others. For one, we teach. We spread knowledge and skills. We foster the love of learning. And we demonstrate the ideals of unconditional love. Any of those things alone make us beautiful.

There are times when we neglect to see the beauty in our students as well. This is especially true of the most troubled student – or the one most challenging to the teacher. The beauty of the child is lost in missing assignments or poor behavior.

The word "ugly" has often been used to describe rude behavior. The word fits. Inappropriate behavior is ugly, but note: when we focus on those ugly features, we prevent ourselves from seeing the beauty in others. Along those same lines, when we act in ways that aren't our best, we don't allow others to see our own beauty.

The most special teachers are the ones that find the beauty in every child. These teachers create an environment where children can self-actualize because they are supported and cared for. Sometimes children have to be taught how to love and respect themselves. We can help children do this by just taking the time to see the beauty in each and every person.

> *"The more man meditates on good thoughts,*
> *the better will be his world and the world at large."*

When we seek to find the good in others, especially children, we make their world a better place. We all need affirmation. We all need love. When we give love, we make other people's worlds a little brighter and a little better. When we give love, we often receive it right back.

When we focus on the good things, the world around us looks better. When our world is brighter, we often share that positivity with others. As such, our happiness and kindness often makes other people's lives better.

In every situation we have a choice. We can choose to see the bad or choose to find the good. We can identify the things that will upset us or we can search to find the things that will uplift us.

> ***"Choose a job you love and you'll never have to work a day in your life."***

If we think about all of the negative aspects of our jobs, we will probably find that we are worn down. When we focus on mandates, requirements, paperwork, salaries, benefits, and the rest, our jobs as teachers becomes work. Those are the things that make a job a job. They wear us down; they wipe us out. But when we focus our energies on the great parts of our jobs – and there are so many and there is so much to cherish – it's not work. When we spend our energies being creative, developing great lessons, making time for children, and giving of ourselves, it's a joy.

Believe it or not, being a principal is not all sunshine and rainbows. Like any job, it can have many frustrations. I try to keep a lot of that to myself. I find that on the days when I focus on the negative aspects of my work, I'm more tired, less happy, and derive less satisfaction from my job. On those days I am "working." But, here's the beautiful thing. I can honestly say that I rarely have to "go to work." Instead, I am fortunate. I go to a school that I love. I interact with children who, by and large, only know about being happy and joyful and full of positive energy. Kids are good at sharing love. The teachers are also positive professionals and the parental community supports them in their outstanding efforts. Confucius is right. On the days I focus on all that is good, I don't work. All the energies I give are returned back to me.

One can never put a value on things such as smiles, appreciation, love, and respect.

Yes, even the nights out – and there are many – aren't always work. When I know that I am bringing joy and happiness to others; I'm not working. Bringing joy and sharing happiness is not a chore. It's what we're there for. That's the joy in what we do.

Confucius was a very smart man – one of the smartest in history. His philosophies resonate today because he understood human nature. He knew, and still teaches us, that our lives can be happy. He knew, and still teaches us, that there is good everywhere.

In the end, it's not complicated. In fact, it's all too simple:

Look for the good – and when you find it, share it, and give it away. It'll come right back.

Quoting Myself

DR. PAUL SEMENDINGER

I like to collect things.

I used to collect baseball cards…lots of baseball cards. When I was younger, I thought that my cards would someday be very valuable. They aren't. Or, at least they aren't as valuable monetarily as I would have hoped as I approach middle-age. (Does anyone want to buy thousands and thousands of baseball cards? Inquire within!)

I used to collect record albums, cassette tapes, and CDs. I don't do that any longer. All of the great music I listen to now rests comfortably in my first generation iPod.

I have a nice collection of old tools that came, mostly, from my grandfather's house. I love my old tools - even if I'm the least handy person…ever. (I'm good at breaking things, not fixing them.)

I used to collect all sorts of old cameras, but now I just focus on one type. In order for me to consider buying an antique camera, the word Semmendinger must appear somewhere on it.

I still collect and hoard books. I love books. I will never have enough room to store all the books in my collection. And I can't wait to get more.

Collecting can become an expensive endeavor.

But I do collect something that is free. I collect quotes. I love a good inspirational quote. When I read or hear something that strikes me, I often write it down and put it in my collection of favorite quotes. I'll never tire of trying to learn from the greatest minds of all time.

Words from the wise can ground me or lift me up. They help me grow spiritually and get me through difficult or challenging times.

IMPOSSIBLE IS AN ILLUSION

They can remind me that I have to work harder and also that I should take time to cherish my accomplishments.

Each year I begin and close the school year with my staff by sharing what is probably my favorite quote of all time. It comes from Theodore Roosevelt:

> *"The credit belongs to those who are actually in the arena, who strive valiantly; who know the great enthusiasms, the great devotions, and spend themselves in a worthy cause;*
> *Who at the best know the triumph of high achievement, and who, at the worst, if they fail, fail while daring greatly, so that their place shall never be with those cold and timid souls*
> *that know neither victory or defeat."*

I usually have only one response to that quote – Wow! It is that quote, possibly among all in my collection, that most reminds me to strive to be my best, in every way, all of the time. I am reminded to fail while daring greatly.

This is what I hope to inspire in others – this ideal that we can all be great if we are willing to take the chance. But even if we don't succeed, that we are better because of the effort.

I often share great quotes with others in letters, e-mails, and in discussions. I post them on my Twitter page. I write about them on my blog. Each Weekly Memo I send to my staff contains a motivational quote. Or two. I always use quotes in my workshop presentations and speeches.

I learn a lot, about life, the world, and myself, by contemplating the great words that others have shared.

There are so many great quotes that I love, that I'd never be able to list them all in any book of any size.

But I'll share just a small number here, words that I live by and think about often (but not always) from some of the greatest minds in history.

"...*dwell in possibility.*"
Emily Dickinson

"*What lies behind you, and what lies in front of you, pales in comparison to what lies inside you.*"
Ralph Waldo Emerson

"*We rejoice in our sufferings, because we know that suffering produces perseverance; perseverance, character; character, hope. And hope does not disappoint us.*"
Romans, 5:3-5

"*The only way to define your limits is by going beyond them.*"
Arthur C. Clarke

"*With malice toward none, with charity for all, with firmness in the right as God gives us to see the right, let us strive on to finish the work we are in...*"
Abraham Lincoln

"*Bid me run, and I will strive with things impossible.*"
William Shakespeare

IMPOSSIBLE IS AN ILLUSION

"There will be days when I don't know if I can run a marathon. There is a lifetime knowing I have."
Anonymous

"Today I consider myself the luckiest man on the face of the earth."
Lou Gehrig

"We choose to go to the moon in this decade and do the other things. Not because they are easy, but because they are hard."
John F. Kennedy

"This is the day that the Lord has made; Let us rejoice and be glad in it."
Psalm 118:24

"Pain is temporary, pride is forever."
Anonymous

"Go For It."
Rocky Balboa

My family knows that I frequently repeat my favorite quotes from movies time and time again.

There are times when people will ask me a question and, instead of a serious answer from me, they get a movie quote in return. Most often I quote from the Rocky movies. I talk like Rocky a lot. (My family has just learned to live with this.)

(As an aside, this is a true story... I have the ability to talk and sound just like Rocky Balboa. As I stated, I often do that at home and with friends. It's just what I do. I don't think I can help it at times. Unfortunately, this sometimes rears its head in other places. One day, at work, a student came up to me in the hall and said, "Hello." I responded, in my Rocky voice, "How ya' doin?" The child, a second grader, looked up to me and said, "I didn't know you could speak Italian.")

My habits aren't always productive. Sometimes when I quote Groucho Marx people think I'm trying to be insulting. I'm not. I'm actually trying to be funny. Yet more than a few people have been taken aback when I've used a Groucho line.

I try not to quote Groucho too much. Sometimes it's not funny.

I have always been in awe of the great writers and thinkers whose words are repeated over and over to help motivate or lift others up. In that light, I've always wished that people would read or hear my words and... quote me.

And then one day after I posted something on Twitter, one of my followers made a graphic of my quote. Then she made a few more.

I was being quoted!

To my amazement, people liked some of my quotes and re-tweeted them.

I wondered if people like me were adding my quotes to their collections.

As such, since this is my book, I figured it would be fun to take a moment and shed all aspects of modesty, step up, be a little pretentious and... quote myself.

IMPOSSIBLE IS AN ILLUSION

Here then, are some of my favorite lines that I've written. Not all come from this book. And this is an informal list that is bound to change. Nonetheless, I hope the reader finds some inspiration, motivation...or even wisdom in my words.

(Or, I assume, some readers will just skip to the last chapter.)

"What we have in abundance, we do not treasure."

*"One of the best parts of being a Dad
is being able to work miracles."*

"Live each day with tomorrow in mind."

*"It's not just about competing in races,
it's more about completing them."*

*"When you work hard at your craft, your craft improves.
Eventually, rather than going to your craft, it comes to you."*

"Whenever you get something with no effort, it isn't as much fun."

*"Teachers can be the biggest heroes of them all.
When they do the job correctly,
when they give of themselves,
when they use their role to inspire and motivate children,
teachers are the world's greatest super heroes."*

DR. PAUL SEMENDINGER

*"Sometimes the best parts of life,
the times when we really find out who we are,
come from the struggle."*

*"We are more beautiful when we are not perfect.
It is our flaws that give us our character.
It is in admitting and recognizing our flaws
– and fixing them –
that gives us our beauty."*

*"What can I do about RIGHT NOW to make this moment
the very best moment it can be?"*

"Always run with a smile on your face."

"I believe I can do anything. I believe we all can."

"Impossible is an illusion."

"Tomorrow is today."
(I am actually planning for this to be the title of my next published compilation of essays.)

The Search for a Semmendinger Camera

(Bonus Essay)

DR. PAUL SEMENDINGER

NOTE – The following passage was originally written in 1998. This article was published in **_CASCADE PANORAMA_** the newsletter or the Cascade Photographic Historical Society in their January 1999 issue.

I have made some modifications to the original article, but, for the most part, have tried to keep this passage true to its original form.

* * * *

I am a descendant of August Semmendinger, an early camera maker. For the first thirty years of my life I knew little about August Semmendinger and had never seen any of the cameras he made or any of the four patents that he held.

The following is a summary of how I came to find, and own, a Semmendinger camera of my very own.

* * * *

My search for a Semmendinger camera began in my childhood. As a child, I was always fascinated when my grandparents told stories about our family history. When visiting Grandma and Grandpa Semendinger, references were made about my great-great-grandfather, August Semmendinger (with two m's), who was a camera maker in Fort Lee, New Jersey.

Unfortunately, outside of the fact that he was somewhat well-known in his time, not much information about August Semmendinger made it to the present day. Then, in 1979, when I was eleven, my grandpa Semendinger passed away. With Grandpa's passing, many of the family stories about the Semmendingers were lost.

IMPOSSIBLE IS AN ILLUSION

As I grew up, I looked to find many answers about our family's history and I became, over time, the family historian. I asked many questions. I also did as much research on my family's heritage as I was able.

In my research, I discovered that the United States Patent Office was able to send copies of any patent they had on file, so I asked for whatever paperwork they had on August Semmendinger. There was some supposition in the family that August Semmendinger had owned a U.S. patent. A short time later, a large envelope arrived in the mail containing copies of three of August Semmendinger's patents. (I later learned he had a fourth U.S. patent.)

Later, when my grandmother was moved to an assisted living facility, I became the possessor of the family documents from August Semmendinger. There wasn't much, mostly just a few old letterheads. I still did not have a great deal of information about August Semmendinger or his camera manufacturing business.

In our quest for more family history, my father and I traveled to areas in Bergen County, New Jersey that might provide answers to some of our questions. We visited an old cemetery in Edgewater that is located in the shadow of the former Alcoa plant. The cemetery was in disrepair when we visited it. We found some family headstones, but could not locate August Semmendinger's.

This was the sum total of my knowledge on August Semmendinger until I purchased a computer and discovered the Internet. This was when the Internet was in its infancy.

One day I typed "Semmendinger" into a search engine. I was shocked, and then thrilled, when I found an actual web site that housed photos of one of August Semmendinger's cameras. For the first time in my life, I actually saw what a Semmendinger camera looked like.

DR. PAUL SEMENDINGER

I immediately e-mailed the owner of the website to inquire about the camera. I asked him if he was willing to sell the camera (he was not) or if he knew of any other Semmendinger cameras. He told me that he knew of only one other Semmendinger camera in the world, and that it was in Europe. Still, I was enthralled. I now knew there were old Semmendinger cameras out there; how many, I did not know. I began to dream of one day owning one of my own.

Not long after, a friend recommended eBay, to me. (Remember, this was written in 1998!). Through eBay, I started to search for all sorts of collectibles, but I never imagined I'd find a Semmendinger camera there. I did start to learn about camera collectors though.

In August, 1998, I stumbled upon the homepage of Pacific Rim Camera. Since they sold antique cameras, I decided to e-mail them asking if they had any Semmendinger Wet Plate cameras. I also asked if they knew of anyone who could help me in my quest to possibly purchase an original Semmendinger camera.

Pacific Rim Camera advised me to email a collector named Milan Zahorcak because he was "very involved in that type of market." I immediately followed this advice and e-mailed Milan sharing my story and quest with him.

I was surprised to learn that Milan knew a little bit about the Semmendinger camera. I was getting warmer. Milan noted that a friend of his actually owned a Semmendinger Camera, but that it wasn't for sale.

At this point, I was thrilled just to know that two Semmendinger cameras existed in the USA. While I knew I could not purchase either of them, I continued to hope that there might be more out there.

Soon after came the shocking news I had been waiting for. On Monday, September 21, 1998, less than a month after I originally contacted Pacific Rim Camera, I received an e-mail from Milan stating that he had just found a Semmendinger camera at a camera show in Vancouver, Canada! I was shocked and excited for the possibilities. The bigger surprise was yet to come – Milan Zahorcak offered to work out an arrangement for me to purchase the camera. I could not believe what I was reading!

I asked Milan many questions and shared with him my fears of purchasing an expensive piece of equipment from 3,000 miles away. Milan answered all my questions and alleviated my fears. I told my father of the possibility of owning a Semmendinger camera and he offered to pay half the cost. We were thrilled. I told Milan we would buy it.

Milan was so helpful and trusting throughout this process. In fact, he looked over and cleaned the camera and explained every aspect of it to me. He mailed the camera before I even wrote the check to pay for it and seemed to be as excited as I was to be part of bringing a Semmendinger camera back to its original family – albeit, over 100 years later.

The camera arrived shortly after. My parents came over to witness the unveiling with my wife and children. It was a big event in our family. Milan included directions on how to unpack and assemble the camera. Step by step, very carefully, we opened, unpacked and put together the Semmendinger camera. It was awe-inspiring. There, in my house, through the magic of this new Internet, was a camera made by my great-great-grandfather sent to us by a new friend 3,000 miles away.

For Milan Zahorcak to take a risk and send a camera from Oregon to New Jersey based on a few e-mailed comments shows how wonderful people can be. Milan took a financial risk in sending the camera to a person he did not know and quite possibly would never meet. Yet, he did it to help someone acquire a most valuable piece of family history.

Still today, I owe a great deal to Milan for all his help and kindness.

I believe when you work hard to be kind and sincere, people, most often, return those sentiments to you. There are times when we can make our own happy endings through hard work, perseverance, and kindness. This was one of those times.

* * * *

My quest to learn more about my family's history continues to this day. Every now and then we find surprises: a passage about August Semmendinger in an old book, an old advertisement in period catalog, and occasionally even a camera for sale. To keep all the information about August Semmendinger and his cameras in one place, I created the web page about him (www.semmendinger-camera.com). It's a hobby and a passion to research, discover, and learn about the small histories of the people that came before us and, in their own ways, helped make us who we are today.

I cannot wait for the next discovery!

* * * *

For more about August Semmendinger, his patents, and his cameras, please visit the Semmendinger Camera web page:

www.semmendinger-camera.com

About the Author

Dr. Semendinger has been a passionate child-centered educator for almost 30 years. He first enjoyed a successful career as a middle school history teacher, earning numerous awards including "Teacher of the Year" and the prestigious "A+For Kids" grant before moving on to administration. Dr. Semendinger has served as a high school vice principal, a middle school principal, and is currently the principal of the most wonderful elementary school in the whole world!

Dr. Semendinger has enjoyed working in various professional organizations including serving as the President of the New Jersey Middle School Association. In addition to the above, Dr. Semendinger has worked for the Educational Testing Service (ETS) and he has served as an adjunct college professor at both Ramapo College and William Paterson University.

An enthusiastic presenter, Dr. Semendinger brings his passion for children to his positive, happy, and engaging presentations. As an accomplished public speaker, Dr. Semendinger has successfully presented workshops at many conferences including those run by the New England League of Middle Schools, STEMCON, the New Jersey Middle School Association, the Madison Institute, local ASCD Chapters, and many others.

Dr. Semendinger is also an accomplished writer. In addition to this text, Dr. Semendinger's first novel, *Scattering the Ashes,* will be released in October 2019. In addition, Dr. Semendinger writes picture books. His first picture book series for children features a wonderful character named Principal Sam. Thus far there have been three Principal Sam books: *Principal Sam and the Calendar Confusion, Principal Sam Gets Fit,* and *Principal Sam and the Three Bears.* All have received excellent reviews! Dr. Semendinger's original and unique history of the New York Yankees *The Least Among Them* is currently being queried. In addition to his published writing, Dr. Semendinger is the Editor-in-Chief of Start Spreading The News, one of the most popular blogs focusing on the New York Yankees. Dr. Semendinger's original writing can also be found on www.drpaulsem.com.

Dr. Semendinger leads an active life. He enjoys running and, to date, has completed twenty one marathons including the New York City Marathon seven times. Dr. Semendinger also plays competitive men's softball and enjoys backpacking and hiking. He also plays the saxophone and piano (but wishes his skills in those areas were much (much) better.) (He's working on it.) In his free time, Dr. Semendinger enjoys reading, travel, and passionately rooting for the New York Yankees.

Dr. Semendinger volunteers his time in many ways. Dr. Semendinger was a three-sport coach (baseball, basketball, and soccer) for sixteen years as his children grew up and was also active in the Boy Scouts where he designed and led outings to historical sites that included Gettysburg,

Washington's Crossing, Valley Forge, Philadelphia, Washington DC, and New York's Central Park. Dr. Semendinger has also successfully led two Boy Scout crews through the two-week backpacking experience at Philmont Scout Ranch hiking treks of more than 90-miles.

Dr. Semendinger is a daily contributor to the Radio Home Visitor (WRKC 88.5 FM—Wilkes-Barre, PA) run through King's College. The Radio Home Visitor brings news to shut-ins in Pennsylvania's Wyoming Valley. Each day Dr. Semendinger contributes an inspirational passage to the program.

Readers interested in the history of photography should note that Dr. Semendinger is also a student of wet plate photography. A descendant of the great camera inventor August Semmendinger, Dr. Semendinger takes great pride in maintaining a web page (www.semmendinger-camera.com) that focuses on August Semmendinger's contributions to photographic history. Dr. Semendinger himself is an amateur photographer. He mostly enjoys taking original photographs in New York City.

More than all of this, a family man, Dr. Semendinger enjoys and greatly values the time he can spend as a husband and dad with his wife and three sons. There is nothing he is prouder of than the fact that he is a good dad and husband. This is a man who loves his family.

www.ingramcontent.com/pod-product-compliance
Lightning Source LLC
Chambersburg PA
CBHW071231230426
43668CB00011B/1381